DRAMAS OF SALVATION

by

F. W. DILLISTONE

With a foreword by the Bishop of London

GEOFFREY BLES · LONDON

© F. W. DILLISTONE, 1967

Printed in Great Britain
by Cox & Wyman, Ltd., Fakenham
and published by
GEOFFREY BLES LTD
52 Doughty Street London WC1

First published 1967

FOREWORD

In this beautiful book Dr. Dillistone has done that rare thing, he has provided us with a new approach to the scriptures. He has lifted us above the often dry but necessary details of historical and literary criticism and asked us to consider the Bible as drama. Since the dramatic emphasis is so largely upon the inter-play of personality, it is evident that this approach must bring us very near the heart of religion. Dr. Dillistone is able to draw upon a wide acquaintance with modern plays to illustrate the Biblical text and to sharpen its impact upon our everyday lives. He has provided both interesting and devotional reading for us all.

✠ Robert Londin:

ACKNOWLEDGEMENTS

The author wishes to thank the Cresset Press for their permission to quote from *A View from the Bridge* and *Collected Plays* by Arthur Miller; A. and C. Black for permission to quote from *From First Adam to Last* by C. K. Barrett and Eyre and Spottiswoode for permission to quote from *Voss* by Partick White.

The author is also indebted to the following for short quotations: Austin Farrer *A Science of God?* (Geoffrey Bles); Amos N. Wilder *Early Christian Rhetoric* (S.C.M. Press); G. von Rad *Genesis* (S.C.M. Press); Geza Vermes *Scripture and Tradition in Judaism* (Humanities Press, New York); Erik H. Erikson *Insight and Responsibility* (Faber and Faber); William Barrett *Irrational Man* (William Heinemann); Wilfred Owen *War Poems* (Chatto and Windus); Marc Connelly *The Green Pastures* (Farrar and Reinhart, New York); T. S. Eliot *Four Quartets* (Faber and Faber); E.R. Dodds *Pagan and Christian in an Age of Anxiety* (Cambridge University Press); S. Mowinckel *He that Cometh* (Basil Blackwell); Kay Baxter *Speak what We Feel* (S.C.M. Press) Patrick White *Riders in the Chariot* (Eyre and Spottiswoode); Eric Bentley *The Life of the Drama* (Methuen); Robert Frost *A Masque of Reason* (Jonathan Cape); Archibald MacLeish *J.B.* (Houghton Mifflin, Boston); T. S. Eliot *The Rock* (Faber and Faber); and Morris Engel *The Problem of Tragedy* (Brunswick Press, Fredericton, Canada).

CONTENTS

Preface   9

1 The Bible as Drama   11

2 The Adventure of Faith   24

3 The Ultimate Sacrifice   43

4 The Role of Mediator   62

5 The Drama of the Servant   82

6 He Who Must Die   103

7

PREFACE

Lent has been traditionally associated with two major themes – Conflict and Passion. Both are essential qualities in the life of the drama. It seems appropriate, therefore, to draw upon man's dramatic experience when attempting to suggest lines of thought for Lenten reading.

I have gratefully used the works of experts in the field of Biblical studies as well as of those who have written on the theory of drama. In the main I have tried to present aspects of the inter-relationship between religion and drama (particularly those derived from the Hebraic heritage within the Christian tradition) which have specially interested me and which may, I hope, be of interest to others.

One of the greatest gifts which came to me through more than eleven years of residence in the city of Liverpool was the awareness of the importance of the dramatic element in the life both of the Church and of Society. In the Cathedral, drama had come to be used in the service of religion: in the Playhouse, I received new religious insights through the service of the drama. I think now of friends in the Cathedral company who played their parts – often seemingly minor ones – with extraordinary fidelity and devotion. I think of friends in the Playhouse company who shed new light on the mystery of human relationships by their intense application to their art and by their spirit of dedication to the community. To all such I wish to express my gratitude by offering this little book as an indication of the kind of help I received through their generous friendship and ready co-operation.

I

THE BIBLE AS DRAMA

I

In the 1966 Lent Book of this series Dr. Austin Farrer dealt in his own inimitable way with the fascinating subject of what it means to believe in God in an age which is dominated by scientific thinking and experimentation. Does it mean that we must now try to think of God as handling nature in the way that we do ourselves, only, of course on a grander and more efficient scale? "We men," Dr. Farrer writes, "are constantly trying to humanise our environment and fit it to our minds. We cultivate the fields, we plan the landscape, we domesticate our fellow creatures, we process materials, we build houses and we construct machines. Even where we leave our environment untouched by our hands we want to get it into our heads; and that means fitting unruly facts into the sort of neat schemes men can master." Are we then to imagine God as a super-Planner and super-Technician who can make the most recalcitrant materials shake down at last into the pattern of his grand design?

Such a view, though suggestive up to a point, is rejected as gravely deficient. And its chief deficiency is that it robs men and things of *the freedom to be themselves*. God "does not impose an order against the grain of things; he makes them follow their own bent and work out the world by being themselves. It is no matter of regret to God that the universe is not a piece of streamlined engineering. It is meant to be what it is – a free-for-all of self-moving forces each being itself with all its might, and yet (wonder of wonders!) by their free interaction settling into the balanced systems we know and into the complexities whereby we exist."

To illustrate this way of working from another area of human experience, Dr. Farrer turns to the art of the novelist. "The Creator of the world is not to be compared with those bad novelists who make up the plot of their story first, and force the characters to carry it out, all against the grain of their natures. He is like the good novelist who has the art to get a satisfying story out of the natural behaviour of the characters he conceives. And how does he do it? By identifying himself with them and living them from within." Yet a human author is severely limited – in the number of people with whom he can truly identify himself, in the complexity of natural processes through which his thought can find its way. The Author of Nature, however, is not limited in these ways. "He thinks all the natural processes at any level into being themselves and into running themselves true to type. And yet without faking the story or defying probability at any point he pulls the history together into the patterns we observe."

I have quoted these passages at some length to show how helpful it is to employ analogies from the realm of artistic activity even when the world around us seems increasingly dependent upon scientific knowledge and technological achievements. Dr. Farrer does not hesitate to use scientific concepts and methods in talking about God. He believes that a study of biological evolution can give us authentic knowledge of the way in which the universal Creator is constantly at work. He believes further that we can acquire experimental acquaintance with the work of God by associating our wills with His. Yet from time to time he draws his illustrations and analogies from the realm of the arts – painting, literary composition, the writing of novels – not because activities in these fields are altogether separate from or antithetical to those of the scientist but because, I think, the arts normally lay a greater stress upon *personal* sensitivities and varieties of *personal* relationships than is the case in scientific investigations and explanations. Science has created a kind of stereotype – the cold, detached observer of phenomena: the practical experimenter: the recorder of recurring patterns. On the other hand art has also created a stereotype – the man imaginatively involved: the eye intensely concentrated upon a tiny segment of human experience: the hand or mouth creating original forms. It is not a question of Either-Or. There is a place for each, not only in the understanding of the universe and of human relationships but also in the attempt to bear witness to God – His Name, His Nature, His Purpose, His Salvation.

And amongst the arts, it seems to me, none is more significant at the present time for the carrying out of this latter task than the art of the drama. I have decided to use the dramatic experience and method in speaking about God in somewhat the same fashion as Dr. Farrer used the scientific method in his essay. He described his own approach to theology as empirical, as an appeal to observed facts, as a testing of theories, as an examination of reasons for thinking that God exists. If it does not sound too pretentious, I should describe my own approach, at least in this particular book, as empathetic, as appealing to certain records of dramatic human experience, as examining recurring patterns of human relationships, as seeking to see the redeeming activity of God manifested in the midst of archetypal human situations. We are right to use scientific language and concepts as we try to speak about God and Nature, God as Creating, God as Fulfilling. We are equally right, I believe, to use dramatic language and concepts as we try to speak about God and Man, God as Redeeming, God as Perfecting. If science can help us to think in a rational and ordered way about the purpose of God in and through the living universe, perhaps the dramatic experience can help us to imagine the nature of God's saving activity in His personal dealings with the sons of men.

Such an approach, it must be said at once, involves one basic assumption. It is that just as any man who takes the trouble – and not only the expert scientist – can observe recurring patterns in the world of natural phenomena so also any serious student of human affairs can detect recurring patterns in man's life in society. To test such an assumption by an appeal to history, though at first sight attractive, is a risky proceeding which can easily arouse all kinds of objections. Are we not making an arbitrary selection of events in the past, weaving them into our own preconceived patterns and then assuming that similar patterns belong both to the social life of our own time and to that of any conceivable future? Personally I believe that a strong case can be made for the existence of recurring patterns in the historical life of mankind but I do not propose to appeal to them in this book. Rather I want to look at the way in which certain art-forms which were constructed in the past and which evoked then such a response as to confirm that they were true to actual human experience, have continued to be reproduced or re-enacted or re-presented in subsequent periods of human history and have repeatedly succeeded in drawing forth from the age in which they have been re-created a similar response of wondering assent. Yes, men have said, though these artistic creations belong to the past they also in an extraordinary way belong to the present. The pattern of human behaviour bodied forth in this story or poem or drama is in a certain sense timeless. Details of setting, tempo, language may be different but the basic structure remains virtually the same and compels our attention and sympathetic response as much today as ever it did.

The most obvious illustrations of this principle are to be found in the abiding power and impact of the great Greek tragedies and of the plays of Shakespeare. A Greek tragedy may be produced today either by directly translating the original verbal and visual symbolisms into their modern equivalents or by using the skeletal framework of the original and clothing it with modern dialogue and action. Oedipus Rex or Hecuba may be presented through the vernacular of any particular country. Alternatively an Anouilh may write his *Antigone* or an Eliot his *Family Reunion* within the structural pattern of Sophocles' *Antigone* or of Aeschylus' *Eumenides* respectively, but with a large freedom of re-interpretation in terms of contemporary situations. Whichever way is used one basic assumption governs the whole dramatic enterprise, namely, that certain patterns of relationships between individuals, societies and extra-human forces, real or imaginary, recur in varied forms within actual human experience and that when these are presented publicly by a creative artist they evoke a ready response just because the audience recognises that what is offered to the imagination is in fact true to life whenever and wherever lived. The play indeed focuses attention upon a particular aspect of human affairs but through this concentrated image some insight at least is granted into those realities which are timeless and universal.

II

Of the continuing appeal exercised by Greek tragic forms there can be no doubt. What can be said, however, about *Hebrew* drama? Were patterns of relationship constantly re-enacted amongst the Hebrews and do they still possess an abiding appeal within our contemporary world? These questions do not allow a simple and straightforward answer but some examination of them may help us to see how our heritage from Jewish sources has been and may still be appropriated within the cultural and religious life of Western Christendom.

At the beginning of an illuminating treatment of *Hebrew Drama* Mr. David Patterson has written: "Unlike the literatures of Greece and Rome, classical Hebrew was never couched, as far as we are aware, in the form of a play. Not that the Bible is lacking in the elements of drama. From the point of view of plot, tension, character and dialogue the narratives of the Old Testament are dramatic in the fullest sense. The very economy of the Biblical story, the skeleton outlines which bite into the imagination and compel the reader to supply the flesh and blood, the stark realities of situation that inflame the emotions to the point of outrage all constitute the very stuff of which dramatic tension is made. . . . Indeed, with the exception of *Psalms, Proverbs, Job, Ecclesiastes* and *Canticles* the Hebrew Bible might be regarded as one long drama with a single theme – how Israel acquired its land, lost it, and then reacquired it – with two principal characters, God and Israel, between whom there is a covenant dependent on the observance of the Law. Nevertheless with the possible exception of *Ruth* with its subtle dramatic tensions and delicately modulated plot and of *Job* which, with its prologue and epilogue and the carefully balanced cycles of long speeches that comprise by far the greater part of the book, certainly bears a highly stylised form, and of the still less likely dramatic structure which some scholars have found in *Canticles*, the Bible displays no trace of conventional dramatic form."*

* David Patterson. 'Hebrew Drama', *J.R.L.B.* 43. 1.

Patterson goes on to discuss reasons for the extraordinary fact that whereas Hebrew history has abounded in dramatic situations, Hebrew literature scarcely yielded a single drama for more than 1,700 years after the close of the Canon. He grants that certain dramatic features were included in the celebration of the festival of Purim but otherwise it appears that no substantial attempt to organise drama in the traditionally accepted sense can be found amongst Jews until the later part of the sixteenth century of our era in Italy, and even since then plays that have been written and acted have mainly been based upon Biblical stories. Yet out of this brief survey of Hebrew drama three points of considerable interest seem to emerge.

In the first place Patterson's suggestion that the Hebrew Bible might be regarded as one long drama has been echoed in the writings of various Christian scholars over the last thirty years. They, on their part, have suggested that the Christian Bible of Old and New Testaments can be regarded in this way. The Old Testament presents a basic structure of call, temporary success, downfall and restoration; the New Testament reveals the pattern in sharper detail in the career of Jesus the Messiah; the history of the Christian Church can be viewed as a constant re-enactment of this same essential drama. Perhaps the clearest exposition of such a view of the Bible may be seen in the Report of the Lambeth Conference of 1958.

Having spoken of the importance of the Bible for all time as lying in the belief "that in Jesus Christ there has been a unique revelation and a unique redemptive act, prepared for by a unique action of the living God in Israel and interpreted by a unique action of his Spirit in the Apostolic Church" it goes on to affirm that in spite of all the variety of the contents of the Bible its unity may be seen "as a drama disclosing the truth about God and man". A whole section is then devoted to an outline of

what is called 'The Drama of the Bible' and of this the first paragraph is couched in the language of the theatre.

"The Hebrew mind sees the story of the world and of mankind
as a drama, in which the author and chief actor is God. It
visualises creation of the universe in a sequence of six scenes
which it calls 'days'. The sixth picture is flashed upon the
screen; it is the appearance of Man upon this planet – Adam, to
use the Hebrew name. It is the epoch of Man, the 'Day' in which
we are still living."

The outline then takes up the story of the patriarchs, the
Exodus, the establishment of the monarchy, the Exile, the
restoration, the tribulations under foreign powers; the coming
of the Messiah, His death and resurrection, the creation of the
new people of God through the Gospel. "Such is the drama of
the Bible. . . . The great Christian doctrines are no more and no
less than interpretations of the Biblical drama which the Church
made under the guidance of the Holy Spirit." And finally it is
suggested that "the Christian Year, which is observed from
Advent to Whitsunday, can be felt by the members of the
Church as a drama in which they themselves are sharing even
now".

But to speak of the whole Bible as drama is to use the actual
word 'drama' in a very general and imprecise way. There is no
thought of a tightly constructed form or of actors being given
words to recite or of a particular audience being gathered to
share in an experience. All that is suggested is that the Bible
possesses a certain unity of structure in which major develop-
ments succeed one another in much the same way as acts and
scenes follow one another in a conventional play. There is a
forward movement towards a *dénouement*, there are in a certain
sense *dramatis personae* and there is a disclosure which is
available for the world to see. Yet if the Bible as a whole is to be

viewed as drama an elaborate process of selectivity and re-arrangement must be undertaken and even then the value is likely to be found more in a general theoretical formulation than in an intense personal participation. The Bible bears witness to a certain series of events which may be regarded as of critical importance in the interpretation of human history. This series may be arranged and subsequently read as literary drama. Only in this sense, it seems to me, can we use dramatic terminology when speaking of the Bible as a whole.

The second point of interest is Patterson's mention of the festival of Purim. We have come increasingly to realise that festivals have always played a most significant part in the history of the Hebrew people. In a certain sense each festival has pro-vided a constant re-enactment of a historical drama. It matters little whether the particular features may or may not have originated in agricultural or pastoral settings. Ultimately each major festival (with the possible exception of the Day of Atone-ment) was associated with certain historical events. Passover re-enacted the deliverance from Egypt: Pentecost the promulga-tion of the Law at Sinai: Tabernacles the journey through the desert and the entrance into the promised land. On each of these occasions ceremonies were enacted and formulae were recited all designed to dramatise the critical event which was being recalled. And at least in ideal all Israel was expected to participate in these experiences. In the words of the Hebrew Haggadah referring to Passover. "In every generation each one of us should regard himself as though he himself had gone forth from Egypt." In every home the essential drama was re-enacted and re-inter-preted and thereby a means was provided of entering ever more deeply into the significance of the saving events.

One major exception I have mentioned – the Day of Atone-ment. Here no specific event was recalled though it seems clear that the festival came into prominence after the return from Exile and may therefore be associated with the need of purification both from those sins which received signal judgement in and through the Exile and also from those defilements which inevitably followed upon closer involvement in the customs and manners of a heathen civilisation. As the record stands however the day is devoted to an elaborate dramatic ritual in which one figure occupies the leading, almost the exclusive, role, though in varying ways those whom he represents are expected to identify themselves in imagination with him. His task it is to slay animals and manipulate their blood in specified ways: in addition to perform a manual act and recite a prescribed formula over a scapegoat before expelling it to its destruction in a desert place. When sacrifices could no longer be offered the record of these dramatic actions could still be read and through prayer and fasting the whole people of Israel could still seek to participate in the annual rite of national purification. Undoubtedly festivals have been occasions of high dramatic significance in Jewish religion.

III

The third reference to drama in Patterson's introductory statement I find the most interesting of all and it is this which I intend to pursue in some detail in the course of this book. This is his description of the narratives of the Old Testament as dramatic in the fullest sense. It could hardly be claimed that this is true of *all* the narratives but it is undoubtedly the case with the stories which relate the all-important events in the lives of its major characters. Adam and Eve, Cain and Abel, Noah and his family, Abraham and Isaac, Jacob and his sons, Moses and

Aaron, Samson and the Philistines, Jephthah and his daughter. Saul and David, David and Absalom, Elijah and Jezebel, Job and his friends, Jonah and Nineveh – all are depicted as involved in situations which are tense, personal, significant. Each stands out as a real character, not least through the words which he uses in the compressed dialogues. If the story as told is too concentrated in form to be suitable for direct acting, again and again it is such as to provide the germ for a play or the framework within which a play could be organised. And in point of fact during the past three centuries, in both Jewish and Christian circles, notable dramas or dramatic operas have been constructed out of the more impressive and appealing of these Biblical narratives.

It is perhaps particularly important to remember that all these Old Testament narratives were originally communicated *orally*. We now *read* them in their terse and polished form. But behind each of these stories we can imagine a long process of telling and retelling, in a way which made each recital something of a dramatic occasion. What Amos Wilder says of early Christian narrators is even more true of ancient Hebrew story-tellers. "When we picture to ourselves the early Christian narrators," he writes, "we should make full allowance for animated and expressive narration. In ancient times even when one read to oneself from a book, one always read aloud. Oral speech also was less inhibited than today. It is suggestive that in teaching the rabbis besides using cantillation also used 'didactic facial expressions', as well as 'gestures and bodily movements to impart dramatic shape to the doctrinal material'."* Thus it is no exaggeration to regard every retelling of one of the great Old Testament stories by a man who possessed the gift of a musical voice and spontaneous mimetic gestures as constituting an impressive dramatic recital. The scene came alive. The audience

* *Early Christian Rhetoric*, 64.

could be caught up into a movement of spontaneous identification comparable to that which happens when any drama of high quality is worthily presented today. The prototype of a modern performance of the St. Matthew Passion was already to be found in the dramatic recital of the story of Abraham and Isaac by some ancient Hebrew narrator.

Moreover these stories, belonging so intimately as they do to the experience of one particular people, can be viewed as bearing witness each in its own way to the total historical drama in which the people of God is involved. This linking together of separated occasions into a single organic whole may be usefully envisaged by drawing a parallel with the common activity of letter-writing. In a notable passage of the works of John Stuart Mill we find him referring to the significance of this form of communication which in his time was becoming increasingly important and efficient.

"It seems to me," he declares, "that there is a very great significance in letter-writing, and that it differs from daily intercourse as the dramatic differs from the epic or narrative. It is the life of man, and above all the chief part of his life, his inner life, not gradually unfolded without break or sudden transition, but exhibited in a series of detached scenes, taken at considerable intervals from one another, showing the completed change of position or feeling, without the process by which it was effected; affording a glimpse or partial view of the mighty river of life at some points and leaving the imagination to trace to itself such figure or scheme as it can of the course of the stream in that far larger portion of space where it winds its way through thickets or impenetrable forests and is invisible: this alone being known to us, that whatever may have been its course through the wilderness, it has had *some* course, and that a continuous one and which might by human opportunity have been watched and discovered, though to us, too probably, destined to be for ever unknown."

The comparison seems particularly apt in the case of the Hebrew people for in a real sense much of their history has been a journey through the wilderness. The forty years wandering has been re-enacted again and again. We see only the glimpse or the partial view of their total history by the aid of the detached scenes which reveal in dramatic form the profound nature of the struggles and questionings which have constituted the inner life of this astonishing people. A single dramatic story can suffice to throw open the windows of the imagination and to enable us to identify ourselves with the *dramatis personae* in their relationships with one another, with the wider community, above all with God. And it is possible for later ages, in the light of widening experience and deepening understanding, to see how a narrative, valid in its own original context, taking on new relevancies in later circumstances, may yet gain a supremely appropriate application in some particular historical crisis. It is my hope to show in some measure how this has been the case by looking at a selection of the most impressive stories of the Old Testament, noticing the way in which appeal may have been made to them in late Judaism or in the New Testament and commenting on some of the uses made of them by artists and writers in more modern times. At best this must needs be a somewhat arbitrary procedure when there are so many possibilities from which to choose. Yet arbitrariness is to some extent held in check by the New Testament itself which, as we shall see, pays special attention to particular Old Testament figures because of the way in which they foreshadow patterns which find their fulfilment in the life and experience of Jesus the Christ. A succession of dramas or dramatic stories from the Old Testament may be seen as having been critically re-enacted in the experience of Jesus Himself and as finding still further possibilities of re-enactment within the new historical circumstances of a later age.

23

2

THE ADVENTURE OF FAITH

I

It is hard to think of any character, whose acts and attitudes
have been recorded in literary form, who has gained such universal acclamation and veneration as has the patriarch Abraham.
In the scriptures of three great religions he is honoured and
celebrated. By later imaginative writers he has been raised to
even greater heights by virtue of his devotion and faith.

Naturally it is in Jewish writings that complete pride of place
is given to the man who came to be regarded as the forefather
of the chosen people. By prophet and chronicler alike he is given
the moving and beautiful title 'The Friend of God'. The wise
man declares that "Abraham was a great father of many people:
in glory was there none like unto him." The historical books
celebrate his faith and courage in leaving the amenities of pagan
civilisation and establishing his claim to dwell in the more
rugged land of Canaan. But his praise is not confined to the Jews.
The Koran also delights to honour the man who was "true in
Faith and bowed his will to God's".

> Who can be better in religion than one
> Who submits his whole self to God, does good,
> And follows the way of Abraham the true in faith?
> For God did take Abraham for a friend.
>
> (Sura IV)

24

In the New Testament we find brief references in Jesus' recorded sayings to the ancestor of His people but it is in the Epistles that he is made the centre of attention and set forth as perhaps the supreme example of a man of faith. Evidently Jewish commentators and theologians were attempting to fill in details in the Old Testament narratives and to draw out lessons for their own people who from the beginning of the second century B.C. onwards were constantly threatened by persecution and even destruction. Paul had been trained in the schools where speculation about Abraham was flourishing and it was only natural that he should add his own tribute of praise to the patriarch from whom he claimed his family descent. But Paul's immediate concern was to see the significance of Abraham for his newly-found faith. If Jesus was indeed the Messiah, if the response of faith to what God had revealed through His Messiah was now the all-sufficient means of gaining salvation, what effect did this have on his veneration for and attachment to such great figures of antiquity as Abraham and Moses. Pure physical descent from Abraham? Meticulous observation of the law of Moses? A proper regard for the exclusiveness of circumcision? All these were now to be counted as loss in comparison with the surpassing worth of knowing Christ Jesus as Lord. Yet this did not necessarily mean that Abraham and Moses ceased to be foci of interest and enlightenment. To discover how the drama of Abraham's career was re-interpreted by early Christian preachers is one of the most interesting exercises within the field of New Testament studies.

II

I have just used the phrase 'the drama of Abraham's career'. In point of fact *two* particular dramas within his career were regarded as of outstanding significance though they could be regarded as coherent parts of the one whole. These two were the Call and the Testing. The Call included the challenge to abandon Mesopotamia and seek another country: the promise of new territory as a home for himself and his descendants: the prospect of universal blessing to be bestowed upon his descendants. The Testing included the uncertainty about offspring: the apparent impossibility of Sarah bearing children: and then, when Isaac was growing to maturity, the demand that the only son should be offered up in sacrifice on the mount of the Lord. Each of these dramatic stories is told with restraint and yet in so tense and personal a fashion that succeeding generations have found it readily possible to become identified in imagination with Abraham in these two dramatic life-struggles.

Probably because different traditions have been combined in the Genesis narrative it is not possible to construct the story of Abraham's decision to set out on his eventful journey in any detailed way. What emerges clearly however is that in response to some call from the Beyond, some constraint which could only be interpreted as a Divine command, Abraham and his family left the relatively advanced civilisation of Mesopotamia and began a trek across the desert towards the land of Canaan. It has been suggested that the general period to which this immigration belongs was one of exceptional turmoil and unrest in the Sumerian Empire. Life and possessions were constantly at the mercy of warlike tribes who, for example, devastated Ur from which Abraham's father is said to have come. But whatever the circumstances may have been in the Haran of Abraham's day, the all-important matter in the narrator's view was that this forefather of the Hebrew people was ready to leave behind the most treasured symbols of human security and commit himself to a pilgrimage into the unknown. As von Rad comments: in his work *Genesis*.

26

"The divine address begins with the command to abandon radically all natural roots. The most general tie, that with the 'land' is named first, then follow, narrowing step by step, the bonds of the clan, i.e. the more distant relatives, and the immediate family. These three terms indicate that God knows the difficulty of these separations; Abraham is simply to leave everything behind and entrust himself to God's guidance. The goal of the migration is 'a land' about which Abraham knows only that God will show it to him." (154.) And at a later point:

"Throughout the entire story one must always remember that to leave home and to break ancestral bonds was to expect of ancient men almost the impossible." (157.)

Anyone who has experienced even the briefest first-hand contact with the peoples of Africa today will recognise immediately how true this comment is to the life of any pre-urban civilisation. 'The land' possesses an extraordinary mystique. To be rooted in a particular section of land gives a sense of dignity and security which can be provided in no other way. Similarly with the bonds of tribe and above all of family: to sever these, to disclaim responsibility for kith and kin, is as momentous as any action that can be imagined. Yet Abraham was so conscious of the beckoning call that, in the entirely simple yet extraordinarily effective words of the writer to the Hebrews "he went out, not knowing whither he went".

Here then we have the first dramatic pattern which was to be re-experienced again and again in Israel's later history. A relative security within an advanced society: a mysterious constraint to abandon home and friends and go out into the 'wasteland' (a literal translation of the word used in Genesis 12. 9): the sense that this constraint derived from the living God, the deity utterly distinct from all the images and idols belonging to the immediate environment: a profound conviction that this God had a rich destiny in store for his people, a destiny in which not only would they themselves discover 'a land' but would also become a source of blessing to all mankind. 'A wandering Aramean was my father' were the opening words of the creed to be recited when the people came into 'the land' (Deut. 26. 5). 'The wandering Jew' has come to be an apt symbol to represent the particular quality of this people in world-history. But the wandering has never been aimless. The precise destination may not have been known. But that the destination was known to God and that He would ultimately guide His people thither are convictions that have never been abandoned even in the darkest days of persecution and distress.

III

To gain some idea of the position which Abraham held in the memory and veneration of the Jews at the beginning of the Christian era one need only glance at the pages of the New Testament. It is true that he does not figure largely in the Gospels but in the writings of Paul and of the author of the Epistle to the Hebrews (both of whom had evidently been steeped in the tradition of the fathers) he stands out as the vivid prototype of the man of faith who was prepared to abandon the old and salute the new at the call of God. Let us look at the ways in which these two writers take up the Old Testament records and apply them to the circumstances of their own day.

The Epistle to the Galatians is a letter which could well have been dictated with the vehemence of an actor engrossed in his part. Paul feels himself to be involved again in the great struggle for freedom which he had so recently fought for himself and which now threatens to overwhelm his Galatian friends. They seem to be on the verge of stepping back into a spurious security which will in fact prove to be a crippling bondage. He speaks of his own experience with passion and relief and then turns to the figure whom all Jewry venerated and whose standing before God as His Friend was never open to question.

What then was the secret of Abraham's acceptance by God? A faithful observance of some strict code of conduct? By no means. "Abraham believed God and it was reckoned to him as righteousness." That is to say, Abraham responded to God's new revelation with courageous faith and active commitment and God, by accepting his trust, declared him openly to be a man in whom He was well pleased. To live according to law inevitably leads to bondage and even slavery. To live according to promise opens the door to freedom and new life.

Faith and promise are dominant categories of the Epistle to the Galatians. Even more are they central and determinative in the Epistle to the Romans. And at the most critical point of his argument, when Paul is declaring that all, literally all, can be restored to a right relationship with God by committing themselves in faith to Christ Jesus, he turns aside for what is in our version a whole chapter in order to appeal to what stands written about Abraham and in order to show that the fundamental pattern already exemplified in Abraham's experience has reached its supreme fulfilment in and through the Christian gospel. Now all who share the faith of Abraham are assured of sharing in the promise made to him. Abandoning the past they can go forth into a future bright with hope and irradiated by the promise of sharing in the glory of God.

In a very real sense Abraham's departure from his original home was a death. He was willing to die to the familiar, the secure, the natural ties of kinship, the prospect of bequeathing to a son what he had been able to improve during his own lifetime. He died to them all. He cast himself upon God, the God, Paul writes, "who quickens the dead and calls into being the things which do not exist". Not only did Abraham experience a death in leaving his homeland. He was virtually at the point of death so far as his own and his wife's physical resources were concerned. Yet the promise still beckoned him on. So, in Paul's magnificent phrase, hoping against hope he gave God the glory being firmly convinced that what God had promised he was able also to perform. He went out into the wasteland – another death – and thereby marked out a way which Jesus Himself was to follow before, being raised from the dead, He brought justification to all men.

In a striking section of his book *From First Adam to Last* Professor C. K. Barrett sketches an illuminating contrast between the story of Adam and that of Abraham. "Adam," he writes, "was placed by God in a situation which, on God's own authority, guaranteed his life and future. It was for Adam to take God at His word and live obediently and trustfully in the situation in which God had placed him, looking to God, as well he might, for the continued supply of all good things. This, as we know, Adam did not do. He doubted God's power and willingness to give him all that he regarded as good; he sought security for himself, and expressed this rebellious and self-seeking temper in an attempt to establish a wisdom and power-for-life that should make him independent of God.

"Abraham found himself in a situation that appeared far less favourable. Instead of being placed within a 'promised land', a garden automatically supplying every need, he was summoned to cross the desert to an unknown country. He was given a promise of life perpetuated in an enduring family, but he was given this promise in circumstances that, so far from favouring, plainly contradicted the possibility of its fulfilment. Wherever

30

Adam looked, his eyes met instances of God's power and favour; for Abraham there was nothing but apparent denial of God's concern for him. Nevertheless it was Abraham who gave glory not to himself but to God, by recognising that God truly was God, able to bring being out of non-being and life out of death; who took due account of all the unfavourable circumstances, yet remained confident that God could and would fulfil his word. Adam sought life for himself in defiance of God's way, and fell out of life into death; Abraham in a situation marked only by death placed the issue of life in God's hand and received life" (35f). Throughout this extract it would be entirely appropriate to substitute 'Everyman' for Adam, 'the man of faith' for Abraham. Everyman-we-I-cling to the outward and visible, the sensible and tangible signs of security, identity, continuity; the man of faith listens for, looks towards, the mysterious sybmols of wholeness, fulfilment, reconciliation, and rejoices in the prospects and promises of God.

IV

If the drama of Abraham's journey into the unknown figures prominently in the writings of Paul, it becomes even more conspicuous in the fascinating letter of the unknown writer to the Hebrews. Whatever complications the Epistle may hold in its detailed expositions, the main situation with which the writer was seeking to deal is quite plain. He was related by ties of affection and interest and concern with a community of Christian people who were losing their first enthusiasm, taking things for granted, slipping from their moorings, becoming sluggish in the race of life, even giving up in despair. In face of such a situation the qualities which he passionately desires to re-create or at least to re-invigorate are faith and patience and hope. The means by which above all he will attempt to achieve such a result is by reminding his readers of dramatic events in the earlier history of the people of God, of the heroic exploits of men of faith in former ages and of the altogether representative and inclusive activities of Him who is the Son of God, the great High-Priest, the Captain of Salvation and the author and finisher of faith. Within this programme it is not surprising that Abraham plays a notable part and it is of great interest to see how the author deals with the Genesis record.

The first reference to Abraham occurs immediately after one of the most solemn warnings of the whole Epistle. The fearful nature of deliberate apostasy is revealed by describing it as nothing less than a re-crucifying of the Son of God and exposing Him to open contempt. The author cannot bring himself to believe that those who have at any time tasted the good things of God will sink to such a depth of infamy. But the only way to prevent such a disaster is to imitate those who through faith and patience have inherited the promises.

Having said this his mind at once turns to Abraham, the father of the faithful. Here was a man of supreme faith who, having in some way gained the assurance that God would bless him and multiply his descendants, clung to the promise through all disappointments and delays. Having patiently endured he actually obtained the promise – though at a later stage in the Epistle the writer will point out that in reality the promise never gains its complete fulfilment under the conditions of this life. The passage in the eleventh chapter in which he again takes up the theme of Abraham's faith is one of the most eloquent and heartening sections of the whole New Testament. I propose to quote it in full.

"By faith Abraham obeyed when he was called to go out to a

32

place which he was to receive as an inheritance; and he went out, not knowing where he was to go. By faith he sojourned in the land of promise, as in a foreign land, living in tents with Isaac and Jacob, heirs with him of the same promise. For he looked forward to the city which has foundations, whose builder and maker is God. By faith Sarah herself received power to conceive, even when she was past the age, since she considered him faithful who had promised. Therefore from one man, and him as good as dead, were born descendants as many as the stars of heaven and as the innumerable grains of sand by the seashore.

"These all died in faith, not having received what was promised, but having seen it and greeted it from afar, and having acknowledged that they were strangers and exiles on the earth. For people who speak thus make it clear that they are seeking a homeland. If they had been thinking of that land from which they had gone out, they would have had opportunity to return. But as it is, they desire a better country, that is, a heavenly one. Therefore God is not ashamed to be called their God, for he has prepared for them a city."

The first paragraph unveils three separate aspects of the patriarch's faith. First attention is focused on a man who as soon as the call sounded in his ears renounced all visible and tangible securities and took his journey into the unseen and unknown future. Such a call inevitably involved a *separation* – every fresh venture into the unknown involves *some* renunciation of comfort and safety. It also involved a continuing *uncertainty* – the promise was of a place whose location was at first quite undefined. This was true faith – to respond with alacrity and yet to receive no immediate confirmation of the validity of the quest. So the second stage is disclosed. It was to reach the land of the promise, the land which in an altogether special way God had designated for the use of His people and yet to live in it as a sojourner or foreigner, a temporary resident, a tent-dweller, a man still possessing no established city.

For Abraham, Isaac and Jacob alike faith meant that they could enjoy foretastes and foresights of the final inheritance but could never regard this world as their final resting place. Though not actually mentioned by the writer, the story of Lot stands as a constant warning to those who seek to find in the earthly city the final goal of life's quest. Only the eternal city has the unshakable foundations and this city cannot be constructed by man nor can it be reached while he remains a creature of space and time. Abraham, William Manson wrote, "was a displaced person, who wandered with his descendants in an alien environment until he died, and his frail tent-home never ceased to contrast with the city of God's foundation on which at the divine call he had staked his all".

The third stage introduces another figure, Sarah, who, though pictured in the Old Testament as doubtful and even derisive so far as the promise was concerned, is here as it were caught up into Abraham's faith, so that she gains power to conceive and becomes the instrument by which the promise of a seed is fulfilled for her husband. At least there is the suggestion that when a man is sufficiently strong in faith he can inspire those of his immediate circle to share his confidence and thereby to become heirs with him of the final promise.

Having celebrated the patriarch's faith in these glowing terms the writer turns aside to point out the wider significance of the ancient record – and who can doubt that he has in mind those Christians dwelling in the world's metropolis, the 'eternal city' of Rome? They were growing disappointed of their hopes and afraid that after all no permanent blessing was coming to them through their Christian allegiance. Starkly and realistically he reminds them: These all, the great heroes of the past, actually *died* without having experienced the fulfilment of the promises either in space ('the land') or in time (the abiding city). Yet they saw the vision of the eternal reality: they hailed it with a cheer: they exulted in the knowledge that nothing earthly or temporal could finally satisfy. Far from bewailing their lot they gloried in the fact that they were foreigners (displaced persons) and so-journers (resident aliens) within the earthly city. And by so doing they revealed the true nature of their quest. In no way were they concerned to look back nostalgically to the past. Had they set their affections in that direction the way was open for them to have returned at any time. But, according to the definition at the beginning of the chapter, their faith was directed to the invisible and the eternal, to the heavenly country. And that their faith has been accepted and approved by God is evident from the very fact that God has become known under the title: the God of Abraham, Isaac and Jacob. Men of faith such as these constitute the true divine commonwealth. In contradistinction to Rome, the secular city, the seat of the earthly imperium, stands the heavenly city, New Jerusalem, coming down from God out of heaven. It is possible and indeed inevitable for Gods people to be engaged in the affairs of the secular city and of the political state. They dare never forget however that this is not the best of all possible worlds, that it is at best only partial and temporary, and that only by a readiness to fold up the tents aud take again to the road can the Christian be constantly moving towards the city which God has prepared for him.

v

The dramatic pattern set forth in the first part of the Abraham story in the book of Genesis has been reproduced again and again in the history of the people of God. A man, a family, a social group is living an apparently normal existence as a constituent part of a settled community. Then the mysterious disquiet, the scarcely perceptible disturbance, the signs of momentary agitation. Like iron filings when a magnet approaches, the man or the company begins to feel the pull of the unseen and unknown.

'Tis God's voice calls! How can I stay?

But any agitation of this kind begins to produce tension, even pain. The seen and the unseen, the old and the new, are in conflict. At length what we call the breaking-point is reached, the severance of ties with home and family, the launching out into the unknown. Even this is not the end of the stress and the strain. Was the decision right? Has the disruption been justified? Is the hope a chimera? Is the unseen a figment of the imagination? The new environment is hostile, the gains seem to be minimal. Would it be better even now to turn back? Are faith and hope and patience really the noblest ingredients of man's lot?

Hermits and missionaries, the oppressed and the enslaved, the adventurers and the pioneers, all in various ways have left their settled environment and gone out in search of fulfilment. Often this has involved hardship and disappointment but the faithful have persisted and some measure of fulfilment, though seldom in the form that had been anticipated, is granted. But in the very fulfilment lies the further temptation. Will the man of faith settle for half? Or will any partial attainment only serve as a stimulus to press on to further achievements in response to the pull of the infinite?

At earlier stages of history this dramatic pattern has found ample scope for realisation in terms of *outward* space and time. There seemed no limit to the distances which could be travelled or to the time-span within which influences could work themselves out. But our outward world has both expanded and shrunk. For ordinary purposes the globe is one, a single village within which the traveller can move from end to end in a matter of hours. Beyond this globe there are limitless vistas of space and time and man's imagination has already been stirred by the exploits of the space-traveller and the adventures of the space-fiction hero. But it is not easy any longer to enact the drama of the mysterious pull and of the riding forth of the relatively unknown knight of faith and of the painful separation from past securities simply in terms of bodily movement. Rather it appears that the migration must now be in terms of the mind and the spirit and the imagination. The man of faith is the one who refuses to settle for the uniform, the one-track, the automatic, the rigidly mechanical. He believes in the *living* God. And in response to the call of the Spirit of Life, he launches out into the world of the personal in which no issue is strictly predetermined and no advance can mark a final attainment, just because 'the two in inter-relationship' rather than 'the one in single mani-festation' constitutes the pattern of the total structure of a life that is fully human.

Of modern dramatists it is Arthur Miller who seems to me to approach nearest to the Abraham story as it is told in Genesis, Romans and Hebrews. He does not, to my knowledge, mention Abraham in any of his writings but his own Jewish background may have brought about an unconscious sympathy with the forefather of his race. Be that as it may, it is clear that all the plays about which he writes in his introduction to *Collected Plays* are concerned with the way in which man establishes his own identity, commits himself to values which are ultimate, rises above the ordinary routine of existence within a society which is seemingly aimless, governed by a grey necessity and governing all its members with an iron determinism.

His diagnosis of our time, in his introduction to *A View from the Bridge*, sketches the kind of background against which his plays were written.

"The deep moral uneasiness among us," he writes, "the vast sense of being only tenuously joined to the rest of our fellows, is caused, in my view, by the fact that the person has value as he fits into the pattern of efficiency, and for that alone. The reason *Death of a Salesman*, for instance, left such a strong impression was that it set forth unremittingly the picture of a man who was not even specially 'good' but whose situation made clear that at bottom we are alone, valueless, without even the elements of a human person, when once we fail to fit the patterns of efficiency. Under the black shadow of that gigantic necessity, even the drift of some psycho-analytic practice *(and I might add of religious and educational practice)** is towards the fitting-in, the training of the individual whose soul has revolted, so that he may once again 'take his place' in society, that is do his 'work', 'function', in other words, accommodate himself to a scheme of things that is not at all ancient but very new in the world. In short, the absolute value of the individual human being is believed in only as a secondary value; it stands well below the needs of efficient production. We have finally come to serve the machine. The machine must not be stopped, marred, left dirty or outmoded. Only men can be left marred, stopped, dirty and alone. Our pity for the victim is mixed, I think. It is mixed with an air of self-preserving superiority – we, thank God, know how to fit in, therefore this victim, however pitiful, has himself to thank for his fate. We believe, in other words, that to fit into the patterns of efficiency is the ultimate good and at the same time we know in our bones that a crueller concept is not easy to arrive at. . . . So long as modern man conceives of himself as

* My italics.

38

valuable only because he fits into some niche in the machine-tending pattern he will never know anything more than a pathetic doom." (11-12.)

Miller's shortest, and in many ways most unassuming play is, he confesses, the one that he loves best. In *A Memory of Two Mondays* he tried, he says, to define for himself the value of *hope*. Nothing, in a sense, could be more dull and ordinary than the scene of the play and the events which it celebrates. It is a warehouse dealing with spare parts for automobiles. There is the endless routine, packing, dispatching, travelling to and fro to work, eating and drinking:

> It's like the subway;
> Every day I see the same people getting on
> And the same people getting off
> And all that happens is that they get older, God!
> Sometimes it scares me; like all of us in the world
> We're riding back and forth across a great big room
> From wall to wall and back again.
> And no end ever! Just no end!

These are the words of the young boy, Bert, and it is Bert who is to break out from the iron necessity of this environment. He is not a great hero, he is certainly not a prig who thinks himself superior to the others. Actually his going forth will hardly cause a ripple in the static pool of warehouse life. But he is determined to assert a different kind of value.

"Bert," Miller has written, "is that young fellow who shares the lives of his compatriots but, at the same time, sees a little further than they. He feels the pathos of their lives and he, unlike them, cannot accept this as the ultimate finality. He wants of life some sense of ecstasy, some union of himself with an ongoing, rising comradeship.

"A routine existence, which accepts the apparent aimlessness of life, is not good enough for him. He wants to assert himself — to test his strength — to add his hand to the creation of justice where there is no justice and he wants to win some recognition of his existence from a world that does not see him even though it pays him." The altogether significant thing about Bert is that he 'presumes to hope' (and we hear echoes of Abraham who 'in hope believed against hope'). "He has no logical right to believe that people, or the world can, in fact, ever rise above necessity, above routine, above the meaningless, ongoing nullity of existence. Nevertheless his spirit insists that things be otherwise." He does not despise those who stay on and endure in the drabness of the weekly cycle. They on their part allow him to go with scarcely a regret. Yet the play ends with one of his workmates humming almost unconsciously

> . . . in the ranks of death you will find him
> His father's sword he has girded on
> And his wild harp slung behind him.

In this play the theme is simple, the message obvious. The four other great plays of the early collection are more subtle and complex. Yet in every case the hero is moved by something *more* than the forces — heredity, physical environment, social influences — which have made him. However closely man is measured and systematically accounted for (using Miller's own words) he is *more* than the sum of his stimuli. Not only is he a creature of his environment: he is an exception to it. "All his heroes," Philip Toynbee has said, "are moved by something more than the urge to defend, or improve, or gratify, or assault the society, which they inhabit. All are moved by a longing to be more than they have been, whether they try to achieve this by self-deception (Willy Loman) or by eventual clarity (John Proctor)."

And this longing for *the more* ultimately issues in some kind of *commitment* (another of Miller's favourite words). "For I understand the symbolic meaning of a character and his career to consist of the kind of commitment he makes to life or refuses to make, the kind of challenge he accepts and the kind he can pass by. I take it that if one could know enough about a human being one could discover some conflict, some value, some challenge, however minor or major, which he cannot find it in himself to walk away from or turn his back on. The structure of these plays, in this respect, is to the end that such a conflict be discovered and clarified. Idea, in these plays, is the generalised meaning of that discovery applied to men other than the hero. Time, characterisations and other elements are treated differently from play to play but all to the end that that moment of commitment be brought forth, that moment when in my eyes, a man differentiates himself from every other man, that moment when out of a sky full of stars he fixes on one star."

[And the Lord brought Abraham outside and said, "Look towards heaven, and number the stars, if you are able to number them." Then he said to him, "So shall your descendants be." And he believed the Lord; and he reckoned it to him as righteousness.]

Miller is passionately concerned for 'the more', 'the exceptional', 'the image of a need greater than hunger or sex or thirst, a need to leave a thumbprint somewhere on the world', 'a conflict, a value, a challenge', 'a universal moral sanction', 'an assertion of meaning'. But why can this not be identified with what the Christian calls 'the ground of our beseeching' and 'the drawing of this Love' and 'the voice of this Calling'? Why cannot 'the moment of commitment' be identified with what the

Christian calls 'the response of faith'? Is not the drama of Abraham still being played out by the unknown Berts who are prepared, in their search for 'the more', in their response to the voice of the Calling, to go out, not knowing whither precisely they are to go? At least this may be the first step on the road which leads to fulfilment beyond all ordinary expectation.

3

THE ULTIMATE SACRIFICE

And it came to pass after these things, that God did tempt Abraham, and said unto him, Abraham; and he said, Behold, here I am. And he said, Take now thy son, thine only son Isaac, whom thou lovest, and get thee into the land of Moriah; and offer him there for a burnt offering upon one of the mountains which I will tell thee of.

And Abraham rose up early in the morning, and saddled his ass, and took two of the young men with him, and Isaac his son, and clave the wood for the burnt offering, and rose up, and went unto the place of which God had told him. Then on the third day Abraham lifted up his eyes, and saw the place afar off. And Abraham said unto his young men, Abide ye here with the ass; and I and the lad will go yonder and worship and come again to you. And Abraham took the wood of the burnt offering and laid it upon Isaac his son, and he took the fire in his hand and a knife; and they went both of them together.

And Isaac spake unto Abraham his father and said, My father; and he said, Here am I, my son. And he said, Behold the fire and the wood: but where is the lamb for a burnt offering? And Abraham said, My son, God will provide himself a lamb for a burnt offering: so they went both of them together.

And they came to the place which God had told him of: and Abraham built an altar there, and laid the wood in order, and bound Isaac his son, and laid him on the altar upon the wood. And Abraham stretched forth his hand and took the knife to slay his son.

And the angel of the Lord called unto him out of heaven and said, Abraham, Abraham: and he said, Here am I. And he said, Lay not thine hand upon the lad, neither do thou anything unto him: for now I know that thou fearest God, seeing thou hast not withheld thy son, thine only son from me. And Abraham lifted up his eyes, and looked, and behold behind him a ram caught in a thicket by his horns: and Abraham went and took the ram, and offered him up for a burnt offering in the stead of his son.

I

The first great drama of Abraham's career was the Call. The second was the Testing. The first attained its peak of significance in the moment of commitment: the second in the moment of sacrifice. In the first Abraham was called to cut himself off from his whole past: in the second he was called to cut himself off from the entire hoped-for future. And whereas the basic story which provides the material for the first has to be reconstructed from documents whose details do not easily fit into a consistent narrative, the story from which we derive the second is sharp and clearly-etched in every part to a degree scarcely equalled in any other section of the Old Testament. Von Rad in fact describes it as 'the most perfectly formed and polished of all the patriarchal stories'. Not only does it provide the framework for the drama of Abraham. It constitutes the drama of Israel, of God's Messiah, of the people of God for all time.

In form the story approximates closely to Jesus' parables. Not a word is wasted. Not a single superfluous detail is included. Not a trace of sentiment is allowed to enter. The pace is perfectly controlled – now moving forward rapidly, now slowing almost to a standstill. Where there is scope for unlimited expansion by the imagination the narrative remains silent. When words are spoken they strike us like the sound of a muffled bell. We move forward, as Kierkegaard was to express it, in *fear and trembling* towards the moment of doom.

The earlier record of Abraham before his supreme testing enhances the dramatic power of the story itself. He had obeyed the voice of God in leaving behind his home and family: he had patiently endured hardship and disappointment: at length the longed-for promise seemed to have been fulfilled through the birth of a child. And now all is being snatched away. The only son, the centre of his earthly love and devotion, is to be offered up in sacrifice. And Abraham does not rebel. Quietly and deliberately he gathers the necessary materials, goes forth on his journey, comes to the point of separation from his faithful servants, and begins the *via dolorosa* in company with the beloved son. The dialogue between the two approaches the limit of poignancy. The record of the binding is utterly realistic. Even the story of the abrupt and unforeseen reversal is told with restraint and almost in a matter-of-fact way. The tiny drama is concluded and we are left to ponder on the depths of significance which the drama holds for our understanding of the relations between God and man.

II

The earliest attempts to interpret and apply this drama to contemporary needs are to be found in a fascinating series of Jewish writings dating from roughly the second century B.C. to the second century A.D. As early as the fourth century B.C. the Old Testament Scriptures were assuming a more settled form and the need naturally arose not only to read these Scriptures regularly but also to draw out their significance for the faith and conduct of the people of God. Much of this interpretation was done orally in the Synagogues but some of the more important rabbinic comments were written down and preserved for future generations. It is from these comments that modern authors have drawn material to show how Old Testament stories and regulations were being interpreted and applied by Jewish scholars during the very period when the writers of the books of the New Testament were faced with the task of interpreting these same Old Testament Scriptures in the light of the career of Jesus Himself.

The name given to the sermons or homilies designed to expound the meaning of Old Testament Scriptures and point out their practical relevance was Haggadah. Haggadah were concerned to respect the written records but also to fuse them with life and apply them to new situations and needs. Naturally certain stories became favourites for exposition – and one of these was the drama of what came to be called the Akedah, the Binding of Isaac. Let us look at one of the oldest and most interesting of the Haggadic commentaries still extant. On verses 8 and 10 it reads:

"And Abraham said: The Word of the Lord shall prepare a lamb for himself. If not, my son, you shall be the burnt offering. And they went together with a quiet heart.

"Abraham stretched out his hand and took the knife to kill Isaac his son. Isaac answered and said to Abraham his father: Bind my hands properly that I may not struggle in the time of my pain and disturb you and render your offering unfit and be cast into the pit of destruction in the world to come. The eyes of Abraham were turned to the eyes of Isaac but the eyes of Isaac were turned to the angels of heaven. Isaac saw them but Abraham did not see them. In that hour the angels of heaven went out and said to each other: Let us go and see the only two just men in the world. The one slays and the other is being slain. The slayer does not hesitate and the one being slain stretches out his neck."

The new notes suggested by this commentary are that Isaac was in fact told that he would be the sacrificial victim and that he willingly gave his consent: that he deliberately asked to be bound so that the sacrifice might be perfectly performed and that on account of his filial devotion he was granted a vision from heaven. In other words, instead of being a passive uncomprehending victim as Genesis 22 implies, he is given by the rabbis a full and significant part in the meritorious action.

At the conclusion of the narrative a further development appears. The comment reads thus:

"Abraham worshipped and said: O Lord, You are He that sees and is unseen! I pray: all is revealed before You. It is known before You that there was no division in my heart at the time when you told me to offer Isaac my son, and to make him dust and ashes before You. But I departed immediately in the morning and did your Word with joy and I fulfilled it. Now I pray for mercy before You, O Lord God, that when the children of Isaac come to a time of distress, You may remember on their behalf the binding of Isaac their father and loose and forgive them their sins and deliver them from all distress so that the generations which follow him may say: In the mountain of the Temple of the Lord Abraham offered Isaac his son, and in this mountain – of the Temple – the glory of the Shekhinah of the Lord was revealed to him."

47

From these and other Haggadic interpretations it becomes clear that in the period immediately preceding the Christian era Jewish commentators were applying the drama of Mount Moriah to the sufferings which had come to their own people as a result of the Maccabean persecutions and continuing foreign oppressions. They read the story and saw Isaac not simply as a passive victim but as one who offered himself gladly in sacrifice and thereby acquired merit for all his descendants. Through his action successive generations of Israel had been saved from final disaster and it was certain that it would avail to bring about the ultimate redemption of all God's chosen people. Indeed so full of virtue was this sacrifice that all animal sacrifices thereafter were only to be regarded as sacramental memorials of the One. "The lamb was chosen," we read in one of the commentaries, "to recall the merit of the lamb of Abraham (i.e. Isaac) who bound himself upon the altar and stretched out his neck for Your Name's sake."

Recognising that there is always a possibility that Christian interpretation of the Death of Jesus may have affected the ideas of certain Jewish commentators of the first and second centuries A.D., Geza Vermes still believes it right to assert that by the beginning of the Christian era "The Akedah (i.e. the drama of the binding of Isaac) was considered a sacrifice of Redemption, the source of pardon, salvation, and eternal life, through the merits of Abraham who loved God so greatly as to offer Him his only son, but principally through the merits of Isaac who offered his life voluntarily to his Creator."* If this was indeed the case, if such ideas were already being freely employed in the interpretation of Old Testament Scriptures, the effect upon the writers of the New Testament as they set about the task of finding meaning in the apparently meaningless act of the crucifixion

* *Scripture and Tradition in Judaism*, 219 f.

of Jesus was likely to be considerable. Are there evidences that this *was* indeed the case?

III

At first sight it may appear that there is little reference to the theme of the 'Binding of Isaac' in the New Testament. Yet certain echoes of the language of the narrative may together constitute an important indication of early Christian use of its dramatic framework. First and foremost we have the magnificent passage in Romans 8, where Paul is moving towards his climax in the concluding verses. Christ Jesus is now spoken of as the 'first-born among many brethren'. To be conformed to His image is now the calling of all God's people. And if this is God's purpose who can possibly hinder or frustrate it? Oppressors, persecutors, mockers? No, "He who did not spare his own Son but gave him up for us all, will He not also give us all things with him"? As we read these words we can scarcely fail to be reminded of Abraham who did not spare his own son, the first-born of his true seed, through whom he was in fact to receive untold blessings. Yet, Paul claims, it was not in fact through Isaac but through Jesus the Christ that the final and unique redemption was achieved: it was through the death of Christ that men could be loosed from their sins and it was through the mediation of Christ that the blessing of Abraham could be granted to all peoples.

There are other echoes of the Akedah in the New Testament. We think of the Gospel accounts of the baptism of Jesus where the phrase, 'my beloved son' quite naturally recalls 'thy beloved son' of Genesis 22. 12. Or again we think of the account in the Fourth Gospel where the title chosen for Jesus is 'the lamb of

God'. Does this not recall Genesis 22. 8, "God will provide himself the lamb for the burnt offering"? As we have seen, Rabbinic commentators were already suggesting that every lamb offered in sacrifice took its virtue from the perfect sacrifice of Isaac. How much more must the offering of the lamb of God be the source and virtue of all earthly sacrifices? Through the self-offering of Christ deliverance from and forgiveness of sin have become available for all mankind. Still further, the fact that Passover had come to be the outstanding memorial celebration of Isaac's self-offering made it apt and appropriate that the new Passover of the Kingdom should be the occasion when the new people of God would celebrate together the memorial of the perfect offering of the Christ.

Two other outstanding references in the New Testament are quite explicit. In the great eleventh chapter of the Epistle to the Hebrews, which speaks so movingly about Abraham's obedience to God's initial Call, what I have called the second drama of Abraham's career is strikingly celebrated.

"By faith Abraham, when he was tested, offered up Isaac, and he who had received the promises was ready to offer up his only son, of whom it was said 'Through Isaac shall your descendants be named'. He considered that God was able to raise men even from the dead; hence, figuratively speaking, he did receive him back." Here the author says nothing of Isaac's part in the drama. The whole emphasis is upon the faith of Abraham who was prepared to obey a command which seemed to lead to the death of all his hopes just because his faith was in a God who could even raise the dead. The promises of God are such that they can penetrate or transcend even the final barrier of death. He, therefore, who offers his all to God through some kind of symbolic death can be assured that he will receive it back from the jaws of death renewed and utterly sanctified. It is not so much the merit of Abraham's action that is in view or the possible far-reaching consequences of his sacrifice. Rather it is the stimulus which such an action provides to all who come after. It stirs them to identify themselves with Abraham in an act of faith which is ready to accept death as the doorway through which God leads men out to a richer and more abundant life. In a slightly different way the author of the Epistle of James seeks to drive home the same message by appealing to the Abraham story. For him faith is only real when it issues in an action as apparently contradictory and extreme as the offering of Isaac. Only at the limit of action does faith receive its final validation. Only at that point is the man of faith judged worthy of the title 'Friend of God'.

I have spoken of the verbal echoes which the New Testament contains of the drama of Abraham's testing. But there is a more indirect parallel which in many ways I find most impressive of all. It is the parallel between Abraham's journey to Mount Moriah and Jesus' journey to Gethsemane. In each case there are companions during the earliest stages. Then comes the first parting, signalling the movement forward to a deeper intensity. Abraham speaks to his young men: Stay here. I and the lad will go yonder and worship. Jesus speaks to the outer circle of his disciples: Sit here, while I go yonder and pray. We now see Abraham going forward with the boy who is innocent of what is about to happen: Jesus goes forward with the three intimates who are similarly unaware of what the night will bring. At length what Abraham does he must do in absolute solitude of spirit: similarly what Jesus does is unknown and unexperienced by any other mortal man. Abraham builds his altar and with fullness of intention makes his offering. Jesus in the silence of the garden sees an altar on which a cup rests, waiting to be drunk: in full surrender he cries: Not my will but Thine be done. Von

Rad uses the phrase 'A road out into God forsakenness' in his commentary on Abraham's testing. The road to Gethsemane seems to belong to the same category. What could be more terrible than to drink alone the cup which mankind has mixed for itself within the economy of God's righteous judgement? But whereas Abraham's ordeal came to its end on Mount Moriah, for Jesus the struggle continued until the final cry of dereliction and God forsakenness was wrung from his lips on the mount of Calvary. In His case there was no apparent reversal or release. He went out into the darkness trusting only in the God who raises the dead.

IV

In the history of the Christian interpretation of the drama of Abraham and Isaac nothing can compare with the passionate intensity of Kierkegaard's meditations brought together into his book *Fear and Trembling*. At a time when, as he says, men were consigning passion to oblivion in order to serve science, when they were also consigning faith to the scrap-heap in order to serve the imposing philosophical system, he was the man who found in father Abraham the supreme exemplar of faith and passion and set to work to restore these energies of the human soul to their true place by entering imaginatively into the drama of the journey to Mount Moriah.

Let us join his company as he writes the opening prologue:

"There was once upon a time a man who had listened in his childhood to the beautiful story of how God tempted Abraham and of how Abraham withstood the test and kept the faith and received his son the second time against all hope. When he grew older he read the same story with even greater wonder: for life had separated what had been united in the pious simplicity of the child. The older he grew, the more often did his thoughts return to this story and each time his enthusiasm increased and yet he understood it less and less. At last he forgot everything else. His soul knew only one desire: to see Abraham; only one regret: that he had not been a witness of the event. His desire was not to see the fair countries of the East or the earthly glory of the Promised Land, or the pious couple whose old age had been blessed by God, or the venerable figure of the aged patriarch, or the exuberant youth of Isaac which God had given to him – for he could see no reason why the same thing should not happen on a barren heath. No, his desire was to follow on his three days' journey, when Abraham rode with sorrow before him and Isaac by his side. His wish was to have been present at the moment when Abraham lifted up his eyes and saw Mount Moriah afar off, at the moment when he sent the asses away and climbed the mountain, alone with Isaac: for his mind was busy, not with the delicate conceits of the imagination, but with the terrors of thought.

"This man was not a thinker, he felt no desire to go beyond faith: it seemed to him the most glorious fate to be remembered as the father of faith, and a most enviable lot to possess it, even if no one knew it.

"This man was not a learned exegete, he knew no Hebrew; perhaps if he had known Hebrew, he would easily have been able to understand the story and Abraham."

The irony of the final sentences of this prologue stands as a warning for all time to Biblical expositors. Since Kierkegaard's days we have made what have seemed to be unparalleled advances in our knowledge of the history and archaeology of the ancient world, of the religious customs of primitive peoples, of the varieties of the forms of sacrificial cultus practised in the

Near East, of the existence even of human sacrifice on special occasions – and we have all too easily assumed that having been armed with this apparatus of learning we should be far better able than our predecessors to understand for ourselves and interpret to others the drama of Genesis 22. Or we have gone to work to construct a system either of the evolution of religious ideas or of the development of ritual practices and have thereby distracted the attention from the utterly central and determinative feature of this particular story – the faith of father Abraham, his passionate, absurd faith, his faith which had no special connection with time or place or even social environment, his faith which came to a passionate concentration in one existential moment, a moment in time yet out of time, a moment which is here, now, always, a moment in which the soul is confronted by God in the terror of the alone, a moment when either faith becomes real or the darkness of night descends. These were the matters which concerned Kierkegaard and it was with these matters in mind that he proceeded to write down the record of his own wrestlings with this incomparable story.

The prologue is followed immediately by four miniature portraits of Abraham which bring to a vivid focus the message of the whole book. It is hardly practicable to reproduce them in their entirety and yet it is difficult to do justice to them by any kind of summary. I shall attempt only to indicate what seems to be the particular aspect of faith which each is designed to represent.

In the first Abraham deliberately makes himself brutal and callous to his son, casting him to the ground and declaring that what he is about to do, far from being a response to the command of God, is simply for his own pleasure because he is in fact an idol-worshipper. Then Isaac terrified cries out to the true God: I have no father on earth, be thou my father. And Abraham rejoices that by blackening his own breast, as it were, to the child, the child has recoiled from him and in its agony has cast itself in faith upon the true and living God.

In the second Abraham simply performs the actions demanded of him, the ram being sacrificed in place of his son. But all is done in an attitude, it appears, of purely passive resignation: in silence, with eyes upon the ground. And when he returns home he cannot forget that God had demanded this of him. His eyes grow dark and he knows no more joy while Isaac prospers as before.

The third brings in the memory of another son. While Abraham is riding away with Isaac his thoughts turn towards Hagar and the son whom he had sent into the wilderness. Then after the drama of Mount Moriah has taken place, we see Abraham riding out again to the mountain and casting himself on his face in order to ask forgiveness for having *wanted* to sacrifice Isaac, for having forgotten his fatherly duty towards his true son. "Frequently he rode this lonely way but he did not find rest."

The fourth shows Abraham preparing the sacrifice, gently and quietly, "but when he turned aside and drew the knife, then Isaac saw that his left hand was clenched in despair and that a shudder passed through his body – but Abraham drew the knife". They returned home but Isaac had lost his faith. "No word of this has ever been mentioned in the world and Isaac never spoke to anyone of what he had seen and Abraham never suspected that anyone had seen it."

These four remarkable variations on the original drama undoubtedly grew out of Kierkegaard's own relationships with Regine Olsen, the woman who for a period was his fiancée but whom he renounced for the sake of a value, an ideal, a calling, a command – no term is adequate to describe the constraint precisely. *"Fear and Trembling,"* he wrote later in his Journals, "actually reproduced my own life." Backwards and forwards he went in imagination from his hero Abraham, stretched to the limit between the claims of his God and the love of his son, and himself, struggling to reconcile his love for Regine with what he deemed to be other more compelling claims upon his allegiance. What were Abraham's thoughts as he rode out on his three-day journey? What was the exact nature of his struggle? To what limit did his faith go? How could he himself follow in the steps of this supreme knight of faith as he called him? These were the questions which tortured and tormented Kierkegaard and out of the agony the four initial dramas of *Fear and Trembling*, together with the dramatic imagery which follows, were born.

Nothing has been easier than to dismiss Kierkegaard as neurotic, half-mad, a perverted genius, a complete bungler in his relations with women. Much has been made of the gloomy, foreboding image of his father, his own deformed body, his sour relationships with the society in which he lived. Yet as Erik Erikson has urged in his lecture celebrating the centenary of Freud's birth, the question has to be asked whether anybody *but* one "at least temporarily afflicted with psychosomatic symptoms, one temporarily sick of his own kind, could or would investigate his own species – provided that he had the inclination, the courage, and the mental means of facing his own neurosis with creative persistence". "A man," he continues, "could begin to study man's inner world only by appointing his own neurosis that angel with whom he must wrestle and whom he must not let go until his blessing, too, has been given."*

If ever a man appointed his neurosis his angel it was Kierkegaard. Only in this case he did it by identifying his angel with that of the patriarch Abraham in the supreme crisis of his life.

* *Insight and Responsibility*, 23.

He felt compelled to follow Abraham, through the desolation of the journey, on to the limit where the knife was unsheathed. Who can doubt that Kierkegaard hoped against hope that somehow, some way, the final reprieve would come to him as it came to Abraham. But the point is that he knew that he must go forward and make the decision of faith even if no outward and visible reprieve should ever be granted to him. He must decide, he must constantly hold to and renew his decision. Only in such a *decision* could life become authentic and gain ultimate meaning.

But the word '*decision*' is fearsome and painful in its derivation. It has to do with cutting through and cutting off. "The drastic Either/Or," Professor William Barrett comments, "had cut through his life as decisively as a sword and no philosopher's balm could remove the pain of loss. The man who has chosen irrevocably, whose choice has once and for all sundered him from a certain *possibility* for himself and his life, is thereby thrown back on the *reality* of that self in all its mortality and finitude. He is no longer a spectator of himself as a mere possibility; he is that self in its reality. The anguish of loss may be redeemed but can never be mediated. Reality for the man who has been called upon to make such a choice is just the reality of his own mortal, finite, bleeding self, and this reality can never be absorbed in a whole in which that finite suffering becomes unreal."*

And for the exteriorisation of this struggle and this decision and this reality no form can compare with the drama. It is not an all-embracing system: it is not a smooth logical sequence. The drama selects the minimum of scenes and events in order to focus attention upon the crises and the decisions and the turning-points where life attains its maximum of intensity and authenticity. Some depth is exposed, some radical tension is brought to

* *Irrational Man*, 138.

decisive action. So in Kierkegaard's variations on the Abraham drama we see conflicting desires and loyalties and constraints working themselves out to a succession of crises within the general framework of Abraham's drama. They are, as it were, brought to the test within the context of the altogether critical act of faith. Aesthetic, ethical and religious considerations are examined in the brilliant light of the ultimate act of faith, the act which defines the individual and his authentic existence. Kierkegaard is not so foolish as to deny that aesthetic, ethical and religious norms are valuable, even necessary for man's ongoing life in society. But his whole concern is for what finally constitutes the individual, for what in the last resort establishes the identity of the self. So his searchlight is directed towards Abraham, the man of faith, the man of action, the man of supreme courage, the man who in his *decision* to obey the call of the highest, even in fear and trembling, provided the archetypal symbol for all time of the true nature and destiny of man.

Kierkegaard cries out again and again in admiration of Abraham. But he also cries out that he cannot emulate his faith. "I am certain that God is love and this thought has for me a fundamental lyrical validity. When it is present, I am unspeakably happy; when it is absent I long for it with more ardour than a lover longs for the object of his desire: but I do not believe, that courage is lacking in me . . . for he who loves God without faith reflects upon himself, but he who loves God with faith reflects upon God. On these heights stands Abraham."

I have attempted to convey something of the quality and flavour of *Fear and Trembling* by means of a few brief comments. But no summary can begin to do it justice. The book belongs to the genre of poetic drama and can neither be systematised nor explained. Yet by its passion and imagination and reflection of inner suffering it throws vivid shafts of light upon the Abraham story and challenges every one who thinks he has faith or that he knows what faith means, to think again and to wrestle again and to dare to venture again in a spirit of awe and godly fear.

V

The most recent use of the drama of Abraham by a modern artist is to be found in Benjamin Britten's widely acclaimed *War Requiem*. As is well-known Britten has daringly juxtaposed the Latin sections of the traditional Requiem with verses taken from the Collected Poems of Wilfred Owen, possibly the most impressive body of poetry to come out of the 1914–18 War.

The Offertory begins with the Boys' Choir singing the petition that the spirits of all the faithful departed may be set free from the mouth of the Lion. The Chorus continues the theme with the prayer that Michael the standard-bearer may represent them in life eternal "which from of old time Thou didst promise to Abraham and his seed". Immediately in poignant and dramatic contrast the soloist sings of Abraham in a very different vein. So Abram rose, and clave the wood, and went,

> And took the fire with him, and a knife.
> And as they sojourned both of them together,
> Isaac the first-born spake and said, My Father,
> Behold the preparations, fire and iron
> But where the lamb for this burnt-offering?
> Then Abram bound the youth with belts and straps,
> And builded parapets and trenches there,
> And stretched forth the knife to slay his son
> When lo! an angel called him out of heaven,
> Saying, lay not thy hand upon the lad,

Neither do anything to him. Behold,
A ram, caught in a thicket by its horns;
Offer the Ram of Pride instead of him.
But the old man would not so, but slew his son, –
And half the seed of Europe, one by one.

This bitter poem is entitled "The Parable of the Old Man and the Young" in Owen's collection. It presents in a terrible way what Owen calls the pity of war. All a poet can do, he wrote, is to warn. But his warnings fell on deaf ears and within little more than a generation the drama was being re-enacted and the sons of Europe were again being slain, this time even the children who knew nothing of the issues involved. And war still continues in the world with chiefly the young being sacrificed on land, on sea and in the air.

Is Owen's diagnosis correct? Is it our pride that is the main culprit in all this? Pride of nation, pride of ideology, pride which will not allow us to admit that earlier plans and policies may have been wrong, pride which seeks at all costs to justify our actions in the eyes of the world at large? Certainly pride was in the ascendant when the chief priests and the Pharisees gathered the council and said, "What are we to do? For this man performs many signs. If we let him go on thus every one will believe in him and the Romans will come and destroy both our holy places and our nation." But one of them, Caiaphas, who was high priest that year said to them, "You know nothing at all; you do not understand that it is expedient for you that one man should die for the people and that the whole nation should not perish."

Our church, our nation, our system of belief: these must be kept sacrosanct, preserved at all costs! To sacrifice some treasured aspect of national or ecclesiastical prestige – this cannot be! Not the Ram of Pride but the Lamb of God! He must die. And by the immeasurable wonder of the Divine irony it was right for Him to die. But what can we who still cling to our pride afford to do save to cry out with fear and trembling:

O Lamb of God that takest away the sins of the world, have mercy upon us?

4

THE ROLE OF MEDIATOR

"Moses was the central figure in the drama of redemption, upon which the national, the religious and liturgical life of the people rested."

C. K. Barrett.

I

Early in the Second Part of Marc Connelly's play *The Green Pastures*, the Lawd discusses with Gabriel the immense problem of what can be done with and for mankind in view of the desperate wickedness which brought about the destruction of the Flood. Suddenly a possible solution suggests itself. In spite of the general apostasy it is clear to the Lawd that every now and then "mankind turns out some pretty góod specimens". There is for example the whole family of Abraham, Isaac and Jacob. So at the divine command they are brought in and the following dialogue ensues:

GOD: Now who do you boys think is the best of yo' men to put in charge down here? You see I ain't been payin much attention to anybody in partic'lar lately.

ISAAC: Does you want de brainiest or de holiest, Lawd?

GOD: I want de holiest. I'll make him brainy.

ISAAC: Well, if you want A Number One goodness, Lawd, I don't know where you'll git more satisfaction dan in a great-great-great-great-grandson of mine.

GOD: Where's he at?

ISAAC: At de moment I b'lieve he's in de sheep business over in Midian County. He's get in a little trouble down in Egypt, but t'wasn't his doin'. He killed a man that was abusin' one of our boys in de brick works. Of co'se you know old King Pharaoh's got all our people in bondage.

GOD: I heard of it. I'm gonter take dem out of it. An' do you know whose gonter lead dem? Yo' great-great-great-great-grandson. Moses, ain't it?

ISAAC: Yes, Lawd.

And the drama continues with most of the Second Part focused upon Moses, his adventures, his achievements, his disappointments and finally his disappearance just as the entry into the Promised Land seems to have been attained.

It is hardly surprising that again and again in history the drama of Moses has brought inspiration and new hope to peoples struggling for freedom and their own social identity. Particularly has this been the case in the chequered history of the Jewish people who have constantly found themselves oppressed and persecuted by nations and empires stronger than themselves. But in the history of Christendom also when minority groups, groaning under some form of tyranny, have become better acquainted with the literature of the Bible no part has exercised a more immediate appeal than that which tells of a child born in circumstances of extreme danger, exalted by a strange irony to a position of high privilege in the oppressor's court, renouncing all in order to identify himself with his persecuted kinsfolk, exiled, apparently forgotten but reborn through the divine disclosure in the burning bush, engaged in a life-and-death struggle with the Pharaoh, leading his people out into freedom yet still driven almost to despair by their fickleness and pusillanimity – the successive stages of the drama have been re-enacted continually in human history and there are no indications that the career of this remarkable man Moses has yet lost its appeal to our modern world.

For example as Part Two of Michael Tippett's *A Child of our Time* opens we see the representative figure of our age, the scape-goat, one part of humanity standing for all, persecuted, execrated, threatened with final destruction. But a boy escapes secretly and is kept in hiding in a great city until at length he makes his bid for the freedom of the 'mother' whom he loves. Throw not your life away in futile sacrifice! Accept the impotence of your humanity! No! I must save her – and he strikes. Then comes the terrible vengeance: bitterness and horror. And at this moment, the moment of darkness and despair, 'A Spiritual of Anger' is heard.

Go down, Moses, Way down in Egypt land,
Tell old Pharaoh, To let my people go.
When Israel was in Egypt's land, Let my people go.
Oppressed so hard they could not stand, Let my people go.
'Thus spake the Lord' bold Moses said, Let my people go,
'If not, I'll smite your first-born dead', Let my people go.
Go down, Moses, 'Way down in Egypt land;
Tell old Pharaoh, To let my people go.

And though 'the child of our time' seems to be outcast and broken there is 'no final grieving but an abiding hope'. The people of God are still on their way over Jordan to the Promised Land, the land of peace.

So the drama of Moses has moved the hearts of men of many

ages, many traditions. In and through this representative figure man's anguished cry for freedom finds an abiding expression. In and through the heights and depths of his career the ecstasies and despairs of all freedom-marchers find a ready key to meaningful interpretation.

II

It would be possible in considering the figure of Moses as a dramatic hero to focus attention upon the incidents leading up to and the consequences resulting from the critical encounter at the place of the burning bush. The symbol of the living fire is one that has captured the imagination of countless searchers for ultimate reality. Here is a symbol of purgation and yet of ennoblement: a symbol of the destruction of evil and yet of the radiation of goodness: a symbol of that which alarms yet also fascinates. It has served as a guiding symbol for the whole Jewish people – a pillar of smoke to lead by day, a pillar of light to lead by night. It has occupied a notable place within the spare symbolism of Reformed Christendom since Calvin adapted it within the form of his own crest – a heart aflame in an outstretched hand

> We only live, only suspire
> Consumed by either fire or fire.

Or it would be possible to reconstruct the drama of Moses' successive encounters with Pharaoh, leading on to the final crisis of the Red Sea when the freedom which seemed firmly within the grasp of the Hebrew slaves could have been snatched away from them even at the eleventh hour. The drama of the Exodus provided the pattern for the freedom songs of the prophets of the Exile and influenced the language and imagery of the writers of the New Testament as they told of the things concerning Jesus Christ. The Passover Lamb had been sacrificed for men. As a consequence Christians could keep festival, rejoicing in the freedom wherewith Christ had set them free. It is indeed this general dramatic aspect of Moses' career which is celebrated in unforgettable words in the Epistle to the Hebrews: this was the man who refused to be called the son of Pharaoh's daughter, choosing to share ill-treatment with the people of God rather than to enjoy the fleeting pleasures of sin. By faith he led the people out of bondage into freedom for he endured as seeing him who is invisible.

But there is a third aspect of the drama of Moses' life which came to be emphasised in late Judaism and occupies perhaps the outstanding place in the New Testament references to his career. It concerns his role as *mediator* between God and the people, a role which involved him in constant tension and brought him to a supreme crisis when there seemed to be no possibility of reconciling the righteous demands of God with the faithless defection of those whom he had been called to represent. In Jewish records, it is true, the tension and struggle in Moses' life are less emphasised. He was mediator in the sense of being the agent by whom God's law was communicated to the nation. He was mediator in the sense of being an advocate and intercessor on behalf of the people. By his prayers they could be sustained in their conflicts with their enemies.

For Christians, however, the question naturally became urgent as to whether Moses *was* the final and all-sufficient mediator. Had the Law given through Moses been intended as a permanent rule of life for the people of God or could it be regarded as a temporary measure ultimately to be superseded by some other agency of the Divine revelation? Had Moses' intercession led always to the vindication of his own people or had their treatment of him been such that the way was left open for the advent of another mediator who would become in an altogether more inclusive way the intercessor, the friend of sinners, the one able to save to the uttermost all who draw near to God through Him?

In the New Testament the most explicit and most extensive commentary on the story of Moses is to be found in the speech of Stephen in Acts 7. In this, Stephen describes how Moses was resisted and thwarted by representatives of his own people in his earliest attempt to secure their freedom: how after he had valiantly led them out from Egypt and mediated to them the 'living oracles' of God they had still refused to obey and had turned back in spirit to the old life of bondage, desiring gods whom they could see and to whom they could offer sacrifices of their own choosing: how when Moses had mediated to them the pattern of the movable tent of worship they had still hankered after a fixed and immovable shrine of their own construction. In fact this leader and mediator appointed by God had been constantly subjected to opposition and misrepresentation by the very people whom he longed to lead out to freedom and true sanctity.

In a more subtle way, by allusion, by indirect reference, by contrast, the author of the Fourth Gospel seems to draw constantly upon the Moses narratives in order to show that what had been achieved and experienced by Moses in partial and shadowy form had been fulfilled and consummated in reality by Jesus, God's Messiah. As Dr. Glasson has shown in his profoundly interesting book *Moses in the Fourth Gospel*, the imagery of the wilderness experiences of the ancient Hebrews is constantly employed by the author as he seeks to bring out the significance of Jesus' own words and actions. But such a use includes a judgement on the

failure of the Jews, both in Moses' and in Jesus' day, to respond
to the leader and to apprehend the significance of his mediatorial
work. All too easily their imaginations were set on the 'meat
that perisheth', on the water that satisfies only for the moment,
on things that can be handled and touched and seen with the
eyes, on words that can be interpreted exactly and literally. In
Jesus' day this was certainly the case. And although the Jews
claimed to be Moses' disciples, Jesus questions the truth of this
claim, declaring that if they genuinely believed Moses they would
believe Him.

The Gospel in fact does not attempt to decry or reject Moses.
He was truly a prophet who had wrestled with the Jews of his
own day, seeking to bring them the knowledge of God through
the Law and to stand as their representative before God through
his intercessions. But what Moses had done as a servant, Jesus
had done as the perfect Son. Therefore those who believed in
Jesus could gain the fullness of the knowledge of God through
His words: those who became His disciples would certainly be
brought into the very presence of God through their com-
munion with Him. On the other hand those who rejected Jesus
would be guilty of even greater sin than those who turned their
backs on Moses. To yearn for the delights of Egypt was bad
enough: to choose deliberately the service of the prince of this
world could only issue in final disaster.

III

What I have called the third aspect of the drama of Moses' life
attains its fullest expression in the record of the worship of the
golden calf. But earlier scenes in the Book of Exodus together
with later scenes in the Book of Numbers can be regarded as

forming Acts 1 and 3 of the drama in which Exodus 32–34 constitutes the central and most significant part. These earlier scenes are concerned with Moses' relationships with the people as a whole and with Aaron in particular: the later again with the people but also with other chosen men who are destined to share his burden and carry on his task.

Suggestions of future conflict may be found even at the time of the encounter with God at the place of the burning bush. Moses hears the call to act as agent of God's deliverance: but what if the people will not listen to me or believe my words? He is aware of the nature of his task as being to speak to Pharaoh and the people in God's name: but what if his own halting speech and lack of eloquence prevent the message from achieving its true effect? The problem of popular unbelief and the tendency of the human heart to cling to outward security, however unpleasant, were to be constantly with him. The difficulties arising from a certain dependence upon subordinates and in particular upon Aaron his brother were to prove a continual source of embarrassment.

In a succession of vivid scenes we learn of the people's bitterness when their lot is made even harder as a result of Moses' demands to Pharaoh. "Then Moses turned to the Lord and said, 'O Lord why hast Thou done evil to this people? Why didst Thou ever send me?'" We see them threatened by the Egyptian armies when they have scarcely begun their journey. "Is it because there are no graves in Egypt that you have taken us away to die in the wilderness? What have you done to us in bringing us out of Egypt?"

We hear their murmurings when they grow hungry. "Would that we had died by the hand of the Lord in the land of Egypt, when we sat by the fleshpots and ate bread to the full!" And again when they grow thirsty. "Why did you bring us up out of

Egypt, to kill us and our children and our cattle with thirst?"
So Moses cried to the Lord, "What shall I do with this people?
They are almost ready to stone me."

Similarly in the Book of Numbers there is a further succession
of scenes in which Moses' struggles with the nostalgia and faint-
heartedness of the people are revealed. "And the people of
Israel wept again, and said, 'O that we had meat to eat! We
remember the fish we ate in Egypt for nothing . . . but now our
strength is dried up and there is nothing at all but this manna to
look at.' Moses said to the Lord, 'Why have I not found favour
in thy sight, that thou dost lay the burden of all this people
upon me? Did I conceive all this people? I am not able to carry
all this people alone, the burden is too heavy for me.'" Again
when the spies sent forward into Canaan return with a report
of war-like tribes being already resident in the land the people
raise a bitter cry: "Would that we had died in the land of Egypt!
Or would that we had died in the wilderness! Would it not be
better for us to go back into Egypt? Let us choose a captain and
go back!" And this is followed by one of the noblest of Moses'
intercessions, concluding with a plea for pardon "Pardon the
iniquity of this people, I pray thee, according to the greatness of
thy steadfast love, and according as thou hast forgiven this
people from Egypt until now."

Such were the dramatic struggles of the wilderness days with
God on one side, the people on the other and Moses in the midst,
pleading and interceding, rebuking and admonishing. But this
was not all. A further series of records unfolds the story of
Moses' relationships with Aaron and Miriam, Eldad and Medad,
Korah and his company, Joshua and Caleb – all occupying
positions of leadership of one kind or another within the community. Clearly there were tensions and disputes, jealousies and
even open rebellions within the ranks of these subordinate

officers. Not the least of Moses' burdens was to maintain order and discipline amongst those who in one instance are simply called 'a rabble'. It is in the tense drama of Exodus 32–34 that all these struggles and conflicts attain their focal expression.

At first reading these chapters seem to lack any clear sequence and to contain units derived from varying sources. Into the historical and literary problems which the narrative raises I do not propose to enter as my concern is with the *dramatis personae* and their relations with one another. These may immediately be defined. God, Moses, Aaron and the people are the chief actors though Joshua and the sons of Levi occupy subordinate roles. The stage is set with Moses still in the mountain, receiving at God's hand the regulations for the religious and social life of his people. But his sojourn in the mountain sanctuary has been a long one. Day after day has passed with no indication of when he will return. Has he deserted the people? Has he been swallowed up in the mysterious conflagration? His deputy, Aaron, begins to lose heart. The people grow restless and when at length they approach him demanding the construction of a visible symbol of strength and protection as an object of worship, he has no spirit to resist. "I said to them, 'Let any who have gold take it off'; so they gave it to me and I threw it into the fire and there came out this calf."

But the celebrations of the new gods have hardly begun when Moses leaves the sanctuary bearing the two stone tablets of the Law and begins to descend the mountain path. Then comes the dramatic moment of truth. What is the noise of the shouting? What is the centre of attraction? The noise is the accompaniment of the ritual dance around the golden bull-calf. In a passionate upsurge of indignation, Moses casts the tablets to the ground and proceeds to mete out punishment to the obvious offenders. But what has Aaron's part been in the whole episode? And what will God's attitude be to the whole future of a people that can so easily return to the old gods?

Two brief scenes are devoted to Aaron's apostasy and his subsequent defence but no hint is given of the way in which his treachery was punished. This man who had served as Moses' mouthpiece and deputy and had been given the responsibility of acting as head of the newly organised priesthood appears in these chapters as a weak, cowardly and evasive character, worthy of little but contempt and obloquy. Yet behind the narrative we may catch fleeting glimpses of conflicts between the pure religion of Israel's God and the nature cults of Canaan: between prophets and priests and Israel itself: between different tribal allegiances: and between a system of religion which depends solely upon verbal oracles and one which demands visible images and symbols. In the drama Aaron is dismissed with biting scorn. But in man's wider religious history the conflict cannot be resolved so summarily. Sight and movement besides hearing and speech must find a place in any fully satisfying religious system.

The chief protagonists in the drama however are God and Moses. We see God reacting in stern judgement towards the defection of the people and threatening to abandon them to their own devices. In their place he will choose Moses as the father of a new and pure seed just as at an earlier stage of world history He had called Abraham to be the father of the faithful. On the other side we see Moses pleading, interceding, seeking a fuller vision of God's glory, above all offering himself as the victim to be punished if only thereby his people can be spared. The dialogues in which Moses sets forth his case in the presence of God are amongst the most moving in the Bible. He seeks to present reasoned arguments: "Why should the Egyptians say, 'With evil intent did he bring them forth to slay them in the mountains and consume them from the face of the earth'?"

"Remember the servants to whom thou didst swear by thine own self and didst say to them, 'I will multiply your descendants as the stars of heaven'." He appeals to God's favour and mercy: "O Lord, let the Lord, I pray thee, go in the midst of us, although it is a stiff-necked people; and pardon our iniquity and our sin, and take us for thy inheritance."

But it is in 32. 30–32 that Moses' intercession reaches the heights. In this tiny drama Moses first confronts the people: "You have sinned a great sin. And now I will go up to the Lord; perhaps I can make atonement for your sin." There is no minimising of the offence. The people's fate hangs in the balance. Then Moses begins to ascend the mountain not as in Abraham's case to offer a son in sacrifice but rather to offer himself – to the limit even of dereliction and damnation. So his broken-hearted prayer begins: "Alas, this people have sinned a great sin; they have made for themselves gods of gold." This is the sin of sins: not lust or pride or sloth or slander but departing from the living God and making images out of the precious gifts of the earth. "But now, if thou wilt forgive their sin –" (the pause is surely the most dramatic in the whole Bible) "and if not, blot me, I pray thee, out of thy book which thou has written." Moses is ready to renounce present privilege and future blessedness if only his people may be restored to the mercy and favour of God.

This willingness of a mediator to go to the limit in identifying himself with his people before the majestic holiness and judgement of God was to form the subject of wondering comments in later Jewish writing. One midrashic passage for example links Moses' intercession with that of the servant in Isaiah 53 who poured out his soul to death and was numbered with the transgressors and took away the sin of many, having made intercession for the transgressors. Another, dealing with the breaking of the Tables of the Law, points out that Moses realised that under the strict law the worship of the Golden Calf would mean the annihilation of the chosen people. Therefore, the Midrash continues, he united his life with theirs and committed the sin of breaking the Tables: whereupon he asked God either to pardon all or to reject him as well – there was now no difference.

Even more striking than these midrashic comments is the outburst at the beginning of the ninth chapter of the Epistle to the Romans. In the earlier part of the Epistle Paul has demonstrated by what seem to be irrefutable appeals to their own Scriptures that the Jewish people are in no better case than their Gentile neighbours – all alike stand guilty before God. Equally impressively he has shown that redemption has been made available to all through the death of Christ Jesus – nothing can now condemn those who have been joined to Him in faith. Yet while all this is true there remains the tragic realisation that apart from a tiny minority the Jews have refused to accept this proffered means of salvation. So Paul suddenly descends from the heights of his exultation in Christ and lays bare another part of his own heart.

"I am speaking the truth in Christ, I am not lying, my conscience bears me witness in the Holy Spirit, that I have great sorrow and unceasing anguish in my heart. For I could wish that I myself were accursed and cut off from Christ for the sake of my brethren, my kinsmen by race. They are Israelites and to them belong the sonship, the glory, the covenants, the giving of the law, the worship and the promises . . . of their race, according to the flesh, is the Christ." All this – and yet they have not accepted the gracious outreach of God in the Christ when He came. "Brethren my heart's desire and prayer to God for them is that they may be saved. I bear them witness that they have a zeal for God but it is not enlightened." Here is something more subtle than idol-worship. It is a written law rather than a golden calf that is the centre of their devotion. But the law can become an idol and so a means of death. Seeking to establish their own righteousness (through the law) they have not submitted themselves to the righteousness of God. And Paul's anguish continues. Loving his people, identifying himself with them, he is ready even to be banished from God's presence if only their eyes can be opened and their consciences enlightened and their sins forgiven.

And surely this was the aspect of the drama of Jesus' own life which left the deepest impression on his followers. He identified Himself with the sick and diseased (who were, it was assumed, in some way under the judgement of God) and, as Matthew quotes, 'took their infirmities and bore their diseases'. He ate and drank with publicans and sinners (who were, it was assumed, in some way outcast from the people of God) and shared the contumely meted out to them by 'the righteous'. He wept over the city of Jerusalem thereby identifying himself with its people in the sorrows so soon to befall them. As the pain and torture of the Cross engulfed Him, as the scorn and insults of the leaders of his own people rained upon him, he made his supreme intercession, Father forgive them: they know not what they do. How natural it was for the evangelist to link Him with the servant of Isaiah 53 and to say that He (more than all others) was numbered with the transgressors. The dramatic pattern of Moses' intercession on Mount Sinai has been fulfilled in word and action through the drama of Mount Calvary.

IV

A most powerful and moving modern re-interpretation of the Biblical drama of Moses is to be found in Schoenberg's opera *Moses and Aaron*. It is not without significance that the form is that of opera rather than of direct play. Moses is to act as the representative of the invisible and inconceivable God. He is to plead passionately for the pure idea, for absolute spirit. And the artistic medium which comes nearest to expressing the ethereal and the non-material is music. Through four three-part chords in the opening bars of the composition, music to which the only human accompaniment is a chorus of six voices using the single vowel 'O', Schoenberg seeks to convey the sense of the single, invisible, utterly transcendent God. Words and actions follow but through endless variations on the initial theme imagination is taken back to the fount of pure spirit, the God beyond all gods, the Absolute, the Eternal.

As the title indicates, the opera has as its central theme the relationship between Moses and Aaron. I have already referred to the hints which the Exodus–Numbers narratives give that in spite of their dedication to the common task these two men were often at variance with one another concerning the leadership, the policies to be employed and the ways in which the being and character of God were to be communicated to the people. It is this tension and conflict which forms the stuff of Schoenberg's drama. Moses and Aaron are at first as closely united as it is possible for two human agents to be. Moses is chosen to hear the voice of the ineffable God: the substance of that which he hears he makes known to Aaron: Aaron in turn is commissioned to speak with power and persuasiveness both to the Egyptian overlords and to the people who are to be redeemed.

But now the divergence and the conflict begins. In the first scene the call of God comes to Moses through the voice from the burning bush. When he hesitates and protests that his tongue is not flexible ('thought is easy: speech is laborious') a new assurance is given.

"Out of this thorn bush, dark before the light of truth fell upon it, so will you perceive my message in everything. Aaron shall be your mouth! From him will your voice then issue as from you comes my voice. Your folk are the chosen ones. They are the folk of God alone. They are thus to know Him, give Him their worship. I shall conduct you forward to where with the infinite oneness you'll be a model to every nation."

In the second scene Moses meets Aaron in the Wasteland. Already however there are indications of divergence. Through their separate scores they carry forward a dialogue in which it is made clear that although they are united in their desire that the divine blessing shall be granted to the chosen people, they are by no means entirely at one in their understanding of the nature of God and of the consequent way in which He makes Himself known to the sons of men. From first to last Moses lifts his eyes towards heaven; upwards to the inconceivable, unimaginable realm of pure spirit: even above this to the utterly transcendent God, beyond all essences and beings, whose voice can be heard by His chosen ones but whose form can never be manifested in human terms. Aaron on the other hand looks for the evidences of God's action in the here and now: for him God is the All-Powerful One who can turn a rod into a serpent and the Nile water into blood: only by miraculous events and signs of omnipotence will the people be persuaded that God is real, that He is indeed active in their midst. And it soon becomes clear that the peoples' hearts are more towards Aaron than towards Moses. They will welcome a God of power, near at hand. To Him they will gladly make their offerings. But Moses like his God seems withdrawn and remote: by dramatic direction he retreats more and more to the background while Aaron increases in the people's esteem.

Between Act 1 and Act 2 there is a dramatic interlude. Voices

come from different directions singing Where is our leader?
Where is Moses? Where is his god? Where is the infinite? And
by the opening of the second Act the stage is set for an open
revolt. Moses has been absent in the mountain for what seems
an interminable period. Aaron and the seventy elders must do
something. There are no commands from on high. The tribes
are quarrelling with one another. Men are even crying out for
Moses' destruction. And Aaron rationalises: "Oh Israel, my
brother Moses tarries where he always is, though he be near to us
or far: he rests upon that summit close to his god. It may be that
he has left us, being far from us. Or may be his god has now left
him, being so near him. Perhaps he approached too near!

"O Israel I return your gods to you and give you to them.
Leave distant things since to you the gods have ever present and
always common substance."

The dam has been opened. Gradually the flood of emotion
gathers strength. Joy leads to exultation, material gifts are out-
poured, the calf is made, the dance begins, all barriers are swept
aside as the people abandon themselves to an orgy of sensuality.
A youth who tries to protest is slain unmercifully. The great
gods of gold and blood give true 'spirit' to their worshippers.
Then at length in Scene 4 comes the dramatic moment of Moses'
return. Seeing the Golden Calf he cries: "Begone! you image of
the impossibility of enclosing the Boundless in a finite image!" –
and the people melt away, as they sing; "The golden light is
quenched. Once again our god cannot be seen. All pleasure, all
joy, all hope are gone, all is once more gloom and darkness. Let
us flee the avenger."

In the final scene of the Act, the inevitable confrontation
between Moses and Aaron sharpens the central issue of the
drama to its most extreme expression. Aaron is unrepentant. No
word had come to him from Moses. His only recourse therefore

was to provide an image for the people. But, Moses replies, his own concern had been with and for *the idea* which is before word and image. The idea has been embodied in the words written on the tables of stone. He *lives* for the idea. But, Aaron responds, "I love this humble folk, I *live* – just for them. You also would have loved them had you only seen how they lived when they dared to see and feel and hope." Again Moses cries, "They must comprehend the idea! They live for that end." But Aaron will have none of it: "What a piteous people, what a folk made of martyrs they would then be! No folk can grasp more than just a partial image, the perceivable part of the whole idea." At least, Moses affirms, he has the tables setting forth the idea: to which Aaron devastatingly replies: "They're images also, just part of the whole idea." Beginning to despair Moses smashes the tables and asks to be relieved of his task. Aaron grows in ascendancy as he reminds Moses of the way in which through outward signs, the fire by night and smoke by day, he has led the people forward. Finally Moses, left alone, sinks to the ground:

"Thus am I defeated, thus all was but madness that I believed before and cannot and must not be given voice. O Word, Thou Word that I lack!"

So to all intents and purpose the drama ends. No music was ever composed for the third act. A libretto exists but it does little more than bring to fuller expession the conflict of the earlier part of the play. Moses regains the ascendancy and by a sustained argument restores the idea to its position of primacy above the image. The supreme danger with an image, it is urged, is that it becomes an end in itself, static, powerless, dependent, pointing to the man who fashioned it rather than to the god it is designed to represent. There is less danger with the word, it is inferred, though even the word must be subordinated to the pure 'idea'. Freedom can only be attained by serving the divine idea and for the communication of this idea no medium is more flexible and dynamic than the word. Aaron's cardinal sin had been that he had 'betrayed God to the gods, the idea to images, the chosen folk to others, the extraordinary to the commonplace'.

Schoenberg wrote as a Jew and sought to re-interpret through modern music and language the heart of Mosaic religion. Yet he was too great an artist to imagine that the vast questions which concern man's religious life and destiny can be answered simply and unequivocally. The struggle between Moses and Aaron represents abiding tensions within the general religious experience of mankind. There is the tension between that which is purely of the spirit, transcendent beyond all conceivable forms, and that which is related to man's common life, immanent, expressed in material forms. Again there is the tension between symbols belonging to the realm of sound-speech, story, music – and those belonging to the realm of sight – paintings, structures, natural objects. Further there is the fundamental tension developed in the opera itself between the idea and the image.

The strength of Moses and of the tradition derived from him has been its intense concentration on the first pole in each of these tensions. There has been a magnificent insistence upon the holiness and the majesty of the one true God: upon the way in which He has spoken to men 'out of the midst of the fire': upon the 'idea' expressed through such a passage as Exodus 34. 6 ff. "The Lord, the Lord, a God merciful and gracious, slow to anger and abounding in steadfast love and faithfulness, forgiving iniquity and transgression and sin, but who will by no means clear the guilty." But with all his admiration for and sympathy with this emphasis, Schoenberg knew well enough that the other pole of the tension could not be completely disregarded. Aaron had a real part to play in the development of Israel's religious life. He may have been misguided, weak, vacillating but his concern for the common man led him to shrink back from the utter formlessness of pure transcendence and to devise forms which could be seen and imaginatively apprehended. There is no need to condone the worship of the Golden Calf if one seeks to do justice to that side of man's nature which can only find satisfaction through sacramental forms and ritual activities.

The drama of the Golden Calf vividly portrays the degradation of man when he abandons himself to perverted forms of religion. At the same time it bears witness to the fact that the generality of men cannot live indefinitely in the rarefied atmosphere of pure ideas and abstract words. As Erik Erikson has reminded us in a striking section of *Young Man Luther*, man needs for his full religious development not only the *guiding voice* but also the *gracious face*. And it is here surely that we recognise so gratefully the fullness and balance of the Christian Gospel. In the beginning was the Word – but the Word became flesh and dwelt among us. The law was given through Moses (and a supreme gift it was) – but grace and truth came through Jesus Christ. And from His fullness have we all received, grace upon grace. Aaron's fumbling efforts to provide the image are understandable. But the Golden Calf is only the reflection of man's baser desires. The true image is the only Son who is in the bosom of the Father. From Him both human words and human images are derived. Through Him the Father has willed to make Himself known.

5

THE DRAMA OF THE SERVANT

I

In the first chapter of his intensely interesting and informative book *Pagan and Christian in an Age of Anxiety*, Professor E. R. Dodds gives an authoritative account of the general attitudes to the world and the human condition which characterised the second and third centuries of the Christian era. It was a time of increasing emphasis upon the contrast, even the antithesis, between the celestial and the terrestrial worlds. The wonder of cosmic space, the sun, the stars, the planets, the bright ethereal sky, was fully recognised. Compared with these, earth seemed but a speck and that a very murky and mutable speck. Within such an environment man's own life, according to Marcus Aurelius, could be regarded as nothing more than "a pinpoint in infinite time, a knife-edge between two eternities. His activities are 'smoke and nothingness'; his prizes are 'a bird flying past, vanished before we can grasp it'." (8.)

If the general condition of man is such, what can be said about the activities with which he busies himself daily? For Marcus they are simply unreal. They have little or no bearing upon the life of the soul as it journeys towards its heavenly home. And this feeling of unreality, Dodds affirms, was fostered by a favourite comparison commonly found in the literature of that time. In this comparison the world was viewed as a stage, men were likened to puppets or marionettes. Even Plato had declared that men and women were puppets chiefly possessing only a small portion of reality. But Marcus went further, comparing the human scene with 'puppets jerking on a string' and the outward life of man as nothing more than a dream and a delirium. All that really mattered was the life of the soul, the inner man, the truly substantial person. And this attitude, so characteristic of pagan leaders of thought, made its appearance even in Christian circles. Augustine could speak of this life as 'nothing but the comedy of the human race' not long after a pagan poet had crystallised the whole outlook in an epigrammatic verse:

> The world's a stage and life's a toy:
> Dress up and play your part,
> Put every serious thought away —
> Or risk a broken heart.*

The world a stage with men as puppets on a string – how great is the contrast between such a conception and the standard outlook of the Old Testament! It is true that there is the occasional metaphor in which the complete power of God to regulate the lives of his creatures is vividly suggested. The potter is working on a vessel of clay: what is to prevent him from casting it aside and beginning afresh? The builder is using stones in his construction: why should he not choose the most suitable and reject the misfits? But these metaphors are of quite limited application. The massive testimony of the Bible is that in the great cosmic drama God and man are acting together. Moreover, it is a real drama in which man possesses a quality and a potentiality of his own. He is not completely independent in the sense of being able to devise his own part impromptu – just as the whim or the mood might take him. On the other hand he is emphatically not

* Cp. Dodds. op. cit., 9 ff.

a puppet to be jerked hither and thither by an entertainer in the wings. And perhaps the greatest safeguard of the limited freedom which the man of the Old Testament enjoys in the adventure of life is his ability to hear and respond to *words*. God is a god who *speaks* to man in the dramatic situation: man is a creature who *speaks* to God in a living dialogue. Not the jerk of a string but the address through the word: not the mechanical reflex but the personal response through the word. This is the drama of the Bible in its most characteristic form.

And if one title more than another can be applied to man in this typical situation it is the title *Servant*. In the drama of life God is the Lord, man is the servant. This is no menial or degrading term. The servant as depicted in the story of Abraham and Eliezer is a man who enjoys his master's full confidence and within certain limits has a wide-ranging freedom of action and decision. Master and servant are united in common tasks and enterprises. A servant may sometimes rise to the more privileged status of friend. A servant may be adopted into the supreme relationship of son. But even then the qualities and attitudes symbolised by the term 'servant' are not to be despised and abandoned. What might be called the central drama of the Old Testament is the drama of the Lord and His Servant. The Lord is the Redeemer; the servant is His chief representative on the world's stage in bringing this redemption into effect.

II

In the Old Testament, Abraham and David are occasionally given the title 'servant': in certain late midrashic passages Isaac is identified with the Servant of Isaiah 53: Moses is referred to again and again as 'My Servant' or 'The Servant of the Lord'.

Indeed it appears that in the historical records it was Moses who was regarded as the servant *par excellence*. In the realm of the imagination however it was the central character in the inspired poems of Isaiah 40–55 who occupied the place of pre-eminence. These dramatic poems paint such a portrait of the true servant of God as is likely never to be surpassed nor forgotten.

I have used the phrase 'dramatic poems'. But it would be equally possible to regard the four poems as successive *acts* in the one drama of the Servant. In the first act (Isa. 42. 1–4) we see the Lord and His Servant in the presence of an unidentified audience. Speaking to them, the Lord declares that He has chosen this particular man, endued him with His own Spirit and that now He regards him as the object of His own special care and delight. Further He defines the servant's task as being that of bringing 'right religion' to the nations. He is not to do this by crying and shouting doom in the market-place. Rather he is to be gentle and patient, mending the bruised reed and tending the dimly burning wick and thereby through message and method commending the good news of the Lord's salvation to the ends of the earth.

The second act (49. 1–6) contains four stanzas in which the servant is the speaker; two others are devoted to the Lord's definition of the servant's vocation. From the moment of his birth he has been dedicated to the task of raising up the tribes of Jacob by restoring them to their true allegiance to the Lord. This task he tried to perform by speaking to them words which like sword or arrow would pierce their complacency and bring glory to the name of God. But he had experienced disillusionment and almost despair. In face of a massive unresponsiveness he had been cast back upon the Lord Himself: he had sought to remain obedient in his service: and even though he seemed to have laboured in vain, it was the question of whether the Lord judged him to have been faithful that finally mattered. And now suddenly there is a new development. Because he *has* been faithful, the Lord is about to entrust him with an even more glorious mission. He is to be made a light to all the nations, a herald of good news to all peoples, a mediator of a salvation which will reach to the ends of the earth.

The first act has shown us the method by which the servant must fulfil his task: the second, the passage through apparent failure to an extension of the tasks. The third (50. 4–9) presents a picture of active opposition and open persecution. The servant speaks again of the nature of his vocation. He has listened with the utmost eagerness and perseverance to the words of his Master. Every morning he has turned to Him for guidance. It has been his constant concern to speak an authentic and enheartening message. But he has been insulted, shamed, tortured. Yet he never turned back, never sought to escape. And now the setting of the drama is suddenly changed to the place where justice is dispensed. The servant confronts his adversaries. Humanly speaking his case seems hopeless. But a Vindicator is near at hand, standing incognito in the court. The servant's confidence rises. He is sure that his enemies will fade away as his Advocate comes to his rescue. Dramatically he concludes:

> He that walks in darkness
> and has no ray of light,
> Let him trust in the name of the Lord,
> and lean upon his God.

Finally all the themes of earlier acts are brought together within the last great act of 52. 13 – 53. 12. In form it is a remarkable symmetry. Two strophes, both at the beginning and at the close, record the Lord's testimony to His servant, a definitive judgement on his work. In between are a series of moving confessions made by an anonymous group designated 'we'. Almost like a Greek chorus, the 'we' fasten their eyes upon the successive stages in the servant's career and by a kind of divine insight estimate its far-reaching significance. His Lord tells of the life poured out even to death as the servant willingly stood amongst the rebellious and made intercession for them: then of the reversal and the exaltation which made him the centre of the wondering amazement of the nations. The 'we' record their own complete change of attitude as they come to realise that the man who by all outward appearances was a hideous and repulsive figure was in fact such because of the load of sins, not his own, that he was willingly bearing, because of the nature of the social environment into which he had willingly entered. "In the poet's thought," Mowinckel writes, "it is not the wrath of God which has imposed the suffering on the servant. But, according to the thought of ancient Judaism, every sin bears within itself the seed of misfortune, a 'fruit' or 'guilt' which in times overtakes the culprit and (or) his family. The sins of Israel are so many and so great, that, if nothing were done to atone for them and to 'purify' the people, she would succumb under the burden of her guilt. Therefore it 'pleased' God in His clemency to establish a purpose or plan, by which a redeemer should bear the burden of guilt which would have been too heavy for the people."*

Such is the four-act drama of the servant. Innumerable attempts have been made to identify the servant by linking him with some historical figure, individual or corporate. Further efforts have been made to systematise its teaching on suffering, redemption and resurrection. But if the record of the servant be regarded as drama these concerns are of only secondary importance. A prophetic author, we may imagine, deeply moved by

* *He That Cometh*, 210.

certain events of his own time, was inspired to present in dramatic form the abiding reality of that which he had seen partially represented in and through the career of an unnamed heroic individual.

What in fact do we know of the historic circumstances? Behind everything stands the bitter, agonising experience of the Exile in Babylon. In the midst of it a new hope had arisen, the hope that Cyrus the Persian conqueror would prove to be God's servant in setting the exiles free and restoring them to their true home. But Cyrus proclaimed his allegiance to the pagan god Bel-Marduk and in no way identified himself with the fortunes of Israel. Though a company of Jews did indeed return to Palestine there was little sign of the general restoration for which the faithful had longed and hoped.

And yet it seems that in this very period, in utter contrast to the military conquerors and political organisers, a man appeared who by his quiet integrity, his humble waiting upon the word of the Lord, his patience in the face of bodily affliction and the contempt of his compatriots, won through to the place of being recognised, at least by a minority, as a true servant of God and a true redeemer of his people. How this recognition found expression we can only guess. Probably not until after his death did the saving and atoning nature of his ministry become fully manifest. But then, inspired by the memory of this man of God, a poet-prophet set out in dramatic form the nature and activity of the authentic servant, thereby creating a portrait of timeless and universal significance.

This process of moving from a particular set of historical circumstances to a far wider application has been impressively described by Arthur Miller in the preface to his Collected Plays to which I have already referred. He is there describing the genesis of his play *All my Sons*. It grew out of a story heard, it seemed, by chance. "During an idle chat in my living-room, a pious lady from the Middle West told of a family in her neighbourhood which had been destroyed when the daughter turned the father in to the authorities on discovering that he had been selling faulty machinery to the Army. The war was then in full blast. By the time she had finished the tale I had transformed the daughter into a son and the climax of the second act was full and clear in my mind." Through his play the full loathesomeness of an anti-social action would be revealed. It would be what he calls a 'prophetic' play, that is a play "meant to become part of the lives of its audience – relevant to both their domestic lives and their daily work, but an experience which widens their awareness of connection – the filaments to the past and the future which lie concealed in 'life'." In other words a simple but profoundly significant incident was destined through the play to expand its influence through ever widening circles of 'life'.

May we not conceive the same kind of process happening in the imagination of the author of the drama of the servant? He knew, perhaps at first hand, perhaps only by reports, of the experience of a prophet who, in Mowinckel's words, "held it to be his mission as a prophet to win his countrymen to true conversion to Yahweh, and a trusting and obedient observance of Yahweh's commands. Like every prophet, he found the work heavy and seemingly hopeless; and sometimes he despaired of everything. But God sustained him, deepened his sense of vocation, and gave him a yet greater goal and wider vision. God did this, too, in the sufferings, the disease and the ignominy which were his lot. He was enabled to maintain his faith and at least discerned that there was a positive divine purpose in his sufferings. They too, being vicarious and redemptive, would serve to bring Israel back."*

* *He That Cometh*, 250.

89

Having known or heard of such a prophet, the poet proceeded to create in dramatic form his universal and timeless representation of the Lord's Servant. He sees in vision a man misunderstood and rejected who yet proved to be the mediator of salvation and restoration not only to Israel but to all mankind. The very horror of his appearance startles those who see him. The very poignancy of his sufferings causes the curious and indifferent to become wide awake as they witness his patience under trial and his unbroken trust in God. So they break out into one of the most moving and compelling confessions in all literature:

He was despised and forsaken of men, a man of pains and acquainted with sickness as one from whom men hide their faces, he was despised and we did not esteem him.

Yet *ours* were the sicknesses that *he* carried, *ours* the pains that *he* bore; while *we* accounted him stricken, smitten of God, and afflicted.

But *he* was pierced for *our* rebellions, he was crushed for *our* iniquities; the chastisement that won our welfare was upon him and by his stripes there is healing for us.

The servant becomes, as it were, the nucleus of a new organism all of whose parts find themselves drawn irresistibly towards the centre. He becomes the focus of a new kind of life in which he stands forth as righteous before the many because he bore their iniquities and interposed for the rebellious. Those who recognise this truth and allow themselves to be identified in imagination and intention with him find themselves walking in the way of health and peace.

In the last resort questions concerning the historical circumstances out of which the drama was born, the identity of the central figure in actual life and the influence of mythological notions of death and resurrection become irrelevant. As in the performance of a drama today, we suspend for the moment questions of this kind. We yield ourselves up to the world of movement and conflict represented on the stage. We share in some measure the emotions and decisions of the chief actors. We proceed through puzzlement to enlightenment, through vacillation to commitment, through deadness of spirit to renewal of hope. The drama of the servant stands as one of the imperishable creations of the human spirit where for the first time the extreme of human dereliction becomes transfigured into God's means of restoring and redeeming a lost mankind.

III

Few subjects have been more strenuously debated within the realm of Biblical studies than that of the influence of the servant-poems on the writers of the New Testament. Did they possess oral traditions or written records which showed that Jesus had identified Himself with the servant-figure openly and consciously? Or that His immediate followers, in seeking to interpret the significance of His death and resurrection had found their clue in the dramatic movement depicted in Isaiah 53? Or did the writers themselves make use of the language and the ideas of the poems as they wrote for their own contemporaries letters and gospels to communicate the things concerning Jesus?

Important and interesting as these questions are it is not my purpose to attempt to deal with them. What is clear beyond doubt is that at a certain stage in the life of the early Church a favourite way of commending the Christian Gospel was by appealing to the imagery of the servant-poems. How far back this practice went can never be certainly ascertained. In particular opinions will continue to differ as to how far Jesus Himself consciously identified His own mission with that of the servant. But in two remarkable instances in the New Testament our attention is turned directly towards the servant-figure. Let us look at the way in which this is done.

The first is to be found in the account of the conversion of the Ethiopian eunuch in Acts 8. This is an extraordinarily vivid story which may well have come straight from the mouth of Philip the evangelist to Luke when the latter was visiting Caesarea. The eunuch was a proselyte to Judaism who had advanced far enough in the new religion to be able to study the Old Testament. But not unnaturally there were passages which puzzled him when he had no one from within the Jewish tradition to guide him.

On the particular day with which the story deals he was wrestling with the words:

> As a sheep led to the slaughter or a lamb before its shearer is dumb, so he opens not his mouth. In his humiliation justice was denied him. Who can describe his generation? For his life is taken up from the earth.

He is obviously fascinated by the picture of the silent sufferer. Who is he? The prophet himself? Some one whom the prophet has known? And Philip seizes the opportunity to tell him of Jesus who had indeed been led as a sheep to the slaughter and whose life had been taken up from the earth. But the narrative gives us no indication of whether other details in the drama were used by Philip in his proclamation of the good news. We are simply told that he *began* with the picture of the silent victim and it is not perhaps unfair to infer therefore that this Scripture was often used as a *beginning* for Gospel preaching. How far the total drama was applied to Jesus and interpreted accordingly we simply do not know.

The second explicit and extended use of the Servant imagery is to be found in 1 Peter 2. 18–25. Significantly this whole passage is addressed to *servants* or slaves who had, perhaps quite recently, become Christians and were chafing under the illtreatment meted out to them by harsh and domineering masters. To all such the author gives a supreme principle of their new life: it is that if they patiently endure pain while suffering unjustly they will certainly win the approval of God: by behaving in this way they are following directly in the steps of Christ Himself.

What after all was the pattern of His life? He was entirely free from sin. He was never guilty of deceit.

> When he was reviled, he did not revile in return; when he suffered, he did not threaten; but he trusted to him who judges justly.
> He himself bore our sins in his own body on the tree that we might die to sin and live to righteousness.
> By his wounds you have been healed.

Here the quotations from Isaiah 53 do not follow the exact sequence of the drama itself, though the total picture of the central figure comes into view. Reviled and afflicted he bore his sufferings in silence without any attempt to retaliate. He carried the sin of many; he brought them healing by his wounds. This is the pattern which the slaves are bidden to keep before their imaginations. By patient suffering they will win the approval of God and may well bring about the redemption of their tormentors.

These two appeals to the drama of the servant are both moving and impressive. But the altogether surprising thing is that they stand virtually alone in the New Testament. We find a phrase here which is a direct quotation from the servant-poems. A phrase there seems to be a verbal echo. But no evidence exists of any frequent reference to the portrait which of all Old Testament pictures seems most suggestive of the actual life-pattern of Jesus Himself. Why this was so we can only surmise. Far too little is yet known of the way in which the poems were applied by the Rabbis of the first century for us to speak with confidence about changes of direction in Christian interpretation during that period. That Jesus in His sufferings and death bore the sin of many is one of the great central affirmations of the New Testament and in this respect His work was a complete fulfilment of that which was dramatically envisaged through the career of the servant. But detailed correspondences between the two figures are seldom emphasised. It was enough, it seems, to declare that Jesus stood firmly in the prophetic tradition (a tradition dramatised for all time in the Isaianic poems), that His career was essentially that of a *servant* and that through His faithfulness even to death men of all nations have found and are finding redemption.

I have said that the two *direct* appeals to the servant-figure are all that can be found in the New Testament. Yet an episode which, in a book written many years ago, J. M. E. Ross called *The Little Drama of the Great Event*, is as vivid a representation of the dignity and redemptive power of service as could well be imagined. Having noted the precise time and setting of the incident the Fourth Evangelist begins to describe it in strangely deliberate and majestic terms:

Jesus, knowing that the Father had given all things into His hands, and that He was come from God and went to God. . . .

"One would think," Ross comments, "that the writer was preparing the way for his supreme assertion of Christ's divinity, but instead, he is preparing the way for his supreme illustration of that spirit of service which ruled the Master's life and death." He laid aside his garments, he girded himself with a towel, he poured water into a basin, he began to wash the disciples' feet and to wipe them with the towel with which he was girded. But this was no merely isolated object lesson. It was a drama expressing the total character of Jesus' mission. He stripped Himself of power and privilege. He poured Himself out in the service of mankind. He purged the deepest recesses of the human spirit. And He said to them:

> Ye call me Teacher and Lord; and you are right for so I am. If I then your Lord and Teacher, have washed your feet, you also ought to wash one another's feet. Truly, truly I say to you, a servant is not greater than his master, nor is he who is sent greater than he who sent him. If you know these things blessed are ye if ye do them.

IV

It is hard to think of any drama of the past twenty years that has more intrigued the would-be interpreter than *Waiting for Godot*. For a while it tended to be viewed in certain circles as a parable of religious expectancy. Then a sharp reaction denied that it contained any vestiges of hope – it could only be viewed as the expression of blank despair in a godless world. What is certain is that it contains many echoes of Biblical incidents and language, above all of the theme of the two thieves on the cross. "Two thieves. . . . One is supposed to have been saved and the other damned. . . . And yet how is it that of the four evangelists only one speaks of a thief being saved? The four of them were there or thereabouts and only one speaks of a thief being saved. . . . Of the other three two don't mention any thieves at all and the third says that both of them abused him." What then determines man's salvation or damnation? Is grace purely fortuitous? Is there any ordered pattern in human affairs or does man go on waiting for – nothing?

These are the dominant questions and leading themes which seem to be in Beckett's mind and I find it hard to see anything more than a faint shadow of the servant-figure which Mrs. Baxter, in her valuable study of modern drama *Speak what we feel*, claims to find in the play. "The tramps together," she writes, "are the spirit of Man. The spirit is spasmodically attentive and expectant of a Saviour. The Saviour comes as it was foretold . . . 'without form or comeliness' (Godichon, godenot). . . . He comes carrying Pozzo's rubbishy gear – 'he hath borne our griefs and carried our sorrows'. He is to have 'a portion divided with the great and shall divide the spoils with the strong' – yes, even if it is only a picnic and the bones of a chicken. The Biblical description of the Suffering Servant fits in every detail the figure of Lucky, this servant of the gross Pozzo who represents all Mankind. And is it hard to agree that 'Lucky' is quite a good modern translation of *Beatus*, the Blessed One, adding to the traditional appellation a twist of sardonic humour apt to our times?" (13–14.)

In succeeding paragraphs further correspondences are suggested. In the part of the play concerned with Lucky, Mrs. Baxter senses a 'total suffering'. And in an age of desolation and grief she finds that this interpretation of the Suffering Servant grips an audience 'with extraordinary power'. It may be so. Certainly *Waiting for Godot* has had an extraordinary effect upon audiences but whether this is due to its revelation of suffering in the person of the wretched Lucky is another matter. Mrs. Baxter has meditated long upon the play and finds herself constantly reminded of Christian themes and enabled to experience in a new way the energy of the Passion of Christ. I can only say that with all my desire and readiness to see the essential Christian drama presented in new and arresting ways through modern art forms, I find it impossible to respond in this way to this particular play of Beckett's. That it is a compelling, original, and profoundly relevant drama I do not doubt, but that it is at heart a re-presentation or re-enactment of the Suffering Servant theme I find it hard to accept.

As I read the record of Lucky I gain the impression of a character who is indeed enslaved and oppressed and ill-treated but who is in his own individuality vicious, ludicrous, abject and incoherent – and none of these adjectives would I readily apply to the figure of the Suffering Servant. It is not a question of asking for exact correspondences but rather of gaining an overall picture. Mrs. Baxter sees a Passion play with Lucky as chief protagonist. I see a play deeply concerned with the human condition, a play of hope deferred, of certainty denied, of progress frustrated. It leaves me finally with a compelling question unanswered rather than with any persuasive indication of an ultimate solution.

For a modern representation of the servant-figure I should more readily turn to the novels of Patrick White. The novel is a comparatively new art form in human history and has really only become possible since the invention of printing and the extension of human literacy. Before that time the spoken word and the mimetic action were all-important and this meant that the dramatic experience was dependent upon a selection of words and gestures which could be spoken and performed within a manageable period of time and within an appropriate setting. But the printed novel could extend to a far longer span of words and could by the use of skilful description become virtually independent of gestures and setting. The experience generated by the novel was not likely to be as intense or as popular in its appeal as that produced by the acted drama but between the two art-forms there is much in common and it is often possible to regard a section of a novel as almost constituting a drama on its own.

The novel, *Voss*, is a kind of dialectical drama which takes us back and forth in imagination between Laura, the woman, wrestling in her spirit with love and anxiety and fear and hope in the narrow confines of a domestic situation, and Voss, the man, wrestling in the flesh with danger and thirst and hostile tribes and dissident companions in the long trek across the desert interior of Australia. But within the drama there are particular scenes in which individual characters reach some apogee of revelation. One such concerns a man who at first sight might be regarded as of minor importance in the total scheme of things. He was Palfreyman, a quiet unassuming member of the expedition led by Voss to explore the interior, his special responsibility being directed to the observation of flora and fauna as he had by profession been an ornithologist. "He was a scientist. Dedication to science might have been his consolation, if it had not been for his religious faith. As it was, his trusting nature built a bridge in the form of a cult of usefulness, so that the two banks of his life were reconciled despite many an incongruous geographical feature, and it was seldom noticed that a strong current flowed between." In the first encounter with Voss he is thus introduced as a man of usefulness (a servant), a man under authority ("It is not a question of my will, Mr. Voss. It is rather the will of God that I should carry out certain chosen undertakings") and yet a man whose spirit was free ("Palfreyman who was frequently very happy in this insubstantial world, walked with the slowness of leisure. But Voss hurried about some business, the wind whipping his trouser legs").

We see him again, as the first part of the journey begins, in company with the uncouth boy who is to be his assistant, at the point "at which they would be offered up, in varying degrees, to chaos or to heroism". The boy sets to work with the packing cases, proud for a little of his strength of body. "But the rather delicate ornithologist remained humble. While the boy's animal nature enabled him to take refuge from revelation in physical strength, the man was compelled to shoulder the invisible burden of the whole shapeless future as his soul had briefly understood it." And this burden, it is soon evident, includes the weights upon the consciences of his fellow-travellers who somehow find themselves drawn to making Palfreyman their confidant and confessor. He may condemn the morality but he loves the man. In contrast to Voss, who nurses his own superiority in all things, Palfreyman is always finding bonds of equality with his fellows. In true humility he receives their attentions and gives them freely of his service.

So the expedition goes forward. Gradually one of the number, an ex-convict, Judd, establishes a certain ascendancy over Voss. Judd is the practical man, the empiricist, strong, shrewd, calculating: Voss is the visionary, proud, almost fanatical in his commitment, contemptuous of all weakness, possessed of a grim determination which nothing can shake. Each gathers to himself those who are drawn by one or the other sets of qualities. And in between is Palfreyman, the mediator, the servant of all, strangely strong though often physically weak. "Grown paler beneath the scales of salt, Palfreyman was sad, who would have melted with other men in love. Whenever he failed, he would blame himself, for he was by now persuaded of his inability to communicate, a shortcoming that made him more miserable, in that the salvation of others could have depended on him. So he would force upon himself all kinds of menial tasks as penance for his disgraceful weakness. He would scour the fat from their cooking utensils with handfuls of the dry, powdery earth; he would strain the scum from any water they found; he even treated Turner, who had broken out in boils, presenting an appearance of the most abject human misery.

"All this the ornithologist taught himself to endure, and the voice of Voss saying:

"'Mr. Palfreyman, in his capacity of Jesus Christ, lances the boils.'"

The journey becomes increasingly difficult. Tensions and jealousies multiply: sickness and disappointment take their toll. But the crisis comes through the worsening relations with the native tribes. Voss is inclined to negotiate with them: Judd is darkly suspicious of them. An axe, a bridle and the one surviving compass had disappeared in the night and Judd was sure that the natives had stolen them. Voss, however, still demands concrete evidence. And finally:

"'As our friend Judd is jealous of my attempts to establish understanding and sympathy between the native mind and ourselves,' Voss observed, 'I will ask Mr. Palfreyman to go amongst them, and investigate this matter of our stolen property. He, at least, is unprejudiced.' 'I am certainly unbiased' he said and smiled thinly. 'I shall go,' he agreed, 'I only hope that I may acquit myself truly,' he added.

"'Here,' said Judd, offering Palfreyman his own weapon.
"'Will you go armed?' asked Voss.

"'No,' said Palfreyman. 'Of course not. Not armed.'

"Palfreyman had begun to walk towards the cloudful of blacks. . . . Over the dry earth he went, with his springy, exaggerated strides, and in this strange progress was at peace and in love with his fellows. Both sides were watching him. The aboriginals could have been trees, but the members of the expedition were so contorted by apprehension, longing, love or disgust, they had become human again. All remembered the face of Christ that they had seen at some point in their lives, either in churches or visions, before retreating from what they had not understood, the paradox of man in Christ, and Christ in man. All were obsessed by what could be the last scene for some of them. They could not advance farther.

"Palfreyman walked on. If his faith had been strong enough, he would have known what to do, but as he was frightened, and now could think of nothing except, he could honestly say, that he did love all men, he showed the natives the palms of his hands. . . .

"Then one black man warded off the white mysteries with terrible dignity. He flung his spear. It stuck in the white man's side, and hung down, quivering. A second black, of rather prominent muscles, and emotional behaviour, rushed forward with a short spear, or knife, it could have been, and thrust it between the white man's ribs.

" 'Ahhhh,' Palfreyman was laughing, because still he did not know what to do.

"With his toes turned in.

"But clutching the pieces of his life. 'Ah, Lord,' he said, upon his knees, 'if I had been stronger.'

"But his voice was bubbling. He had failed evidently. Mr. Palfreyman was already dead when the members of the expedition arrived at his side and took him up. Nor was there a single survivor who did not feel that part of him had died."

So the man who had made himself the servant of all and tried to take at least some of the sufferings of humanity upon himself had failed. Voss and his other companions go forward to their own ultimate destruction in the blinding desert. Yet at the last Voss himself learns what it is to be truly humble. Through the prayers of Laura, through his own suffering and disappointment, through the vision of the true *servant* revealed in Palfreyman's sacrifice Voss himself is redeemed and transfigured into the image of the divine.

If no modern drama suggests itself immediately as having been created in the pattern of the servant-poems, the figure of Palfreyman in *Voss* and equally impressively the figure of Himmelfarb in *Riders in the Chariot*, seem to me to be moulded in the image of the servant. Each is instrumental in achieving, in the dramatic crisis of his life, that redemption of the human lot which comes only from suffering, patiently and willingly borne. After his mock crucifixion, Himmelfarb 'quietly left the factory in which it had not been accorded to him to expiate the sins of the world'. But 'although nobody watched, everybody saw.' And wherever men see, in art or in life, the pattern of suffering service truly enacted, it becomes the more possible for them to see beyond the reflections to the One in whom all such patterns find their integration and fulfilment, the One who came not to be served but to serve and to pour out His own life so that the many might be saved.

6

HE WHO MUST DIE

"A character in a play does not talk merely to show what he is like, nor is he allowed to talk himself out. He is limited in his utterances to what bears on the play as a whole, keeps it moving, advances it just as much as it needs to be advanced, and at the proper rate of speed.

"And this constitutes a supreme idealisation of life, for it signifies a life which had a clear and unitary meaning, a direction, an utterly purposive momentum towards an end. In this respect, dramatic art is one of the great wish-fulfilling dreams, for there is nothing human beings more ardently crave than to be persons in such a drama. In the Middle Ages, it was official doctrine that humanity did belong in such a drama, and so the art of the drama represented a metaphysical fact. But this art has as great a poignancy – or greater – in an age like our own when the universe is generally felt to be unintelligible, amorphous, undramatic. For today art offers the only integrated drama, and we can be persons in a perfectly constructed Action, it would seem, when we read or see a play."

Eric Bentley, *The Life of the Drama*

I

In the magnificent conclusion to his roll-call of the heroes of faith in Jewish history, the writer of the Epistle to the Hebrews exclaims: "What more shall I say? For time would fail me to tell of Gideon, Barak, Samson, Jephthah, of David and Samuel and the prophets," and then proceeds to summarise their exploits before turning the gaze of his readers to the central figure of all, 'the pioneer and perfecter of our faith', whose dramatic acceptance and endurance of the Cross proved to be the means of salvation for all mankind. In my own attempt to describe some of the great dramas of the Old Testament and their modern re-interpretations I too might speak of Samson and Jephthah and Hosea and Job but this I shall do only briefly. I want to join company with the author of Hebrews in directing attention finally to the drama in which the central figure is Jesus Himself.

Samson's life-story is of the very stuff of tragedy. Foreordained to greatness, endued with exceptional physical prowess, maturing in a situation which cried out for dynamic leadership, he yet fell victim to the wiles of a seducer and finally capitulated to his hated enemies. Yet the sparks of faith and courage were never completely extinguished and though blind and alone he succeeded in the end in gaining a more far-reaching victory through his death than through his life.

Such are the bare facts of the record but in the hands first of Milton, then of Handel, these facts were transformed into one of the noblest dramatic poems in our language and one of the finest oratorios of our musical heritage. I say 'transformed' deliberately for the facts in themselves constitute an unlovely story of lust, deceit and vengefulness which lacks all the splendour of the Abraham and Moses narratives. Yet Milton by his sheer artistry of language and form created a drama which has the power to fascinate and move us even when the sentiments contained in it seem crude and repellent.

How poignantly the human condition is symbolised:

> I, dark in light, exposed
> To daily fraud, contempt, abuse and wrong,
> Within doors, or without, still as a fool,
> In power of others, never in my own—
> Scarce half I seem to live, dead more than half.
> O dark, dark, dark, amid the blaze of noon,
> Irrecoverably dark, total eclipse
> Without all hope of day!
> O first-created beam and thou great Word,
> 'Let there be light, and light was over all',
> Why am I thus bereaved thy prime decree?

How deep is the contrition of the desolate hero:

> Nothing of all these evils hath befallen me
> But justly; I myself have brought them on;
> Sole author I, sole cause . . . Let me here
> As I deserve pay on my punishment,
> And expiate, if possible, my crime.

Yet how exultant is the cry of the chorus as they hear the news of Samson's death:

> O dearly bought revenge, yet glorious!
> Living or dying thou hast fulfilled
> The work for which thou wast foretold
> To Israel, and now liest victorious
> Among thy slain self-killed;
> Not willingly, but tangled in the fold
> Of dire Necessity, whose law in death conjoined
> Thee with thy slaughtered foes, in number more
> Than all thy life had slain before.

And how imperishable are the words of the aged father as he gives the final verdict on his son's career:

Nothing is here for tears, nothing to wail
Or knock the breast; no weakness, no contempt,
Dispraise or blame; nothing but well and fair,
And what may quiet us in a death so noble.

It is not the Christian drama of redemption. Rather is it the drama of a man's titanic struggle with 'dire Necessity', the drama of a single supreme act of courage eclipsing all that has been sordid and unworthy. Out of such a drama comes a sense of calm and peace, 'all passion spent', as man realises that God orders all for the best even when his servants fail and betray Him. Milton deliberately set out to write a tragedy according to the Greek model and succeeded marvellously in adapting an Old Testament story to this end. Pity and fear and terror are aroused by Samson's plight and ultimate revenge: they are purged as the spectator moves through the tension of the drama to its final resolution. Though purgation is not salvation it may be the first stage towards it. At least the watcher has his passions reduced to just measure and out of the midst of human sorrows and sufferings finds peace and consolation in the all-wise providence of God.

Beside Samson, Jephthah seems an almost shadowy figure. Little is told us in the Old Testament about his character and exploits but the one major incident that is recorded has captured the imagination of dramatists at various times in human history. In the midrashic literature the daughter's sacrificial devotion was celebrated as comparable to that of Isaac himself. Though Jephthah is depicted as sorrowful, the daughter cries: Who can be sad to die if by that death the people are set free? Art thou unmindful of the things that were done in the days of old when a father laid his son upon the sacrificial altar and the son did not resist but consented to be the victim so that thereby the sacrificer and his offering could rejoice together?

Probably the most notable of all dramas based upon the Jephthah story, however, comes from the Christian Middle Ages. In a deeply interesting broadcast printed in *The Listener* of November 25, 1965, Peter Dronke of Cambridge gave an account of the numerous Latin poems which survive from the twelfth century and in particular of Abélard's dramatic elegy *Planctus virginum Israel*, the lament of the girls of Israel over the death of Jephthah's daughter. "We know almost nothing," he writes, "about this girl from the Bible; there she is given only one sentence to speak. It is Abélard who has created a character whom we might soonest compare with an Iphigenia or Antigone – who might indeed, had he composed on the scale of tragedy rather than lyric *lai*, have attained the stature of such a heroine."

In Abélard's drama it is not in fact Jephthah who is the hero of faith. Rather it is the daughter whose obedience and courage and passion and faith are celebrated to the skies. She longs to be chosen to experience in actuality what Isaac experienced only in anticipation. When her father falters she beseeches him to be a man and to act in such a way as to bring glory both to himself and to her. All she asks is for two months' grace so that her maidens may accompany her to the mountains and bewail her unfruitful maidenhood.

The play draws to its close with two remarkable scenes. First the heroine is prepared for the final sacrificial moment as if she were going forward to her marriage.

One girl hands her linen, moistened with her tears, another holds the crimson silk, wet with weeping. Ear-rings, bracelets, golden rings weigh down her tender young body.

Now she cannot bear the weight of things, the drawn-out

ritual – rising from her bed, she flings the rest away and says: "It is enough for a bride; too much for one who must die." At once she takes the naked sword and hands it to her father. This is the climax. But it is not the conclusion. The daughters of Israel are seen again celebrating the yearly rite. They are torn in feeling between anger at Jephthah who by his action destroyed not only his immediate victim but his people as well and wondering admiration of the daughter who by the nobility of her own sacrifice brought nobility to all who become united with her through participation in the passionate lament.

"Sing, daughters of Israel, remember that glorious girl, sing the peerless girl of our people – we are greatly ennobled through her."

Again this is not the Christian drama of redemption. Rather is it the drama of a maiden's struggle with the inviolability of a vow, the drama of a noble spirit of resignation eclipsing the foolhardiness of a weak man's strategy of opportunism. In his last book *God and Golem Inc* Norbert Wiener warned us against the dangers which beset all gadget worshippers of trying to avoid perilous personal decisions by appealing, like Jephthah, to some random eventuality. And this is a constantly recurring situation in man's journey through time. In Abélard's adaptation of the story folly and suffering are transformed through the celebration of a heroic spirit in an imperishable artistic form.

II

Of all the books of the Old Testament none approaches more nearly to the dramatic form than does the book of Job. It is now generally assumed that the opening chapters 1 and 2 together with the closing section, 42. 7–17, are a literary version of a popular folk-tale which belongs to no particular period of history. In between there are cycles of speeches which are presented in the form of dramatic poetry. Probably these speeches come from more than one author and have been collected and skilfully worked together by an editor. It is therefore possible to regard this remarkable book as offering four dramatic interpretations of a single theme – the problem of human suffering. There is the folk-tale, Job's debate with his three friends, the speeches of Elihu and finally the voice of the Lord out of the whirlwind with Job's response. Only the first of these attempts to present what might be called a solution of the problem. The others in many ways intensify the problem. Yet as can so often happen, through the experience of witnessing a dramatic conflict, the reader who enters with sympathy into the struggle and the debate of the book of Job gains illumination and encouragement for the renewal of his own engagement with the changes and chances of this mortal life.

Whatever may be said and thought about the later debates and the proferred solutions, nothing can detract from the extraordinary dramatic power of the opening chapter. I have always remembered an example of this recorded by the Scottish preacher John A. Hutton in his volume of essays *The Dark Mile*. He tells of a Sunday when he was reading this chapter as morning lesson in a little country church. He had reached verse 13 and was continuing:

And there was a day when his sons and daughters were eating and drinking wine in their eldest brother's house: and there came a messenger unto Job, and said, The oxen were plowing and the asses feeding beside them: and the Sabeans fell upon them and took them away; yea, they have slain the servants with the sword: and I only am escaped alone to tell thee. While he was yet speaking, there came also another and said, The fire of God is fallen from heaven and . . . the sheep. . . . While he was yet speaking, there came also another . . . the camels! and the young men! and while he was yet speaking another . . . thy sons and daughters . . . are dead.

"At the reading," Hutton says, "the little church became still, so that I could scarcely continue. The silence acquired that quality which I have known it to possess in a lonely place at high noon and in great heat, when it makes one afraid. I could not keep my eyes on the printed page but had to raise them. . . . It was with difficulty I resumed."

And he said, Naked came I out of my mother's womb, and naked shall I return thither: the Lord gave and the Lord hath taken away: blessed be the name of the Lord.

"What I felt then was that as I was reading of blow upon blow falling upon the head of a man of Chaldaea thousands of years ago, those simple, thoughtful people were saying to themselves; 'How like life that is.'"

But although we should readily agree that the prologue depicts a scene which is timeless and universal in its appeal, the debates and the arguments of the later chapters, in spite of their vivid imagery and poetic form, do not so easily lend themselves to application within our contemporary scene. And it is not surprising that modern poets and dramatists have sought to use the general setting and circumstances of the book while at the same time creating dialogues more obviously related to our own problems and concerns. Robert Frost attempted this in what must be regarded as one of his less impressive works, *A Masque of Reason*, in which a free-flowing conversation between God, Job, Job's wife and Satan ranges over some of the questions which the Biblical narrative leaves unanswered. The general thesis is that God needed man's co-operation in the task of refuting and subduing Satan. But at one point Job cries:

I am flattered proud
To have been in on anything with You.
Twas a great demonstration if You say so.
Though incidentally I sometimes wonder
Why it had had to be at my expense.

To which God replies:

It had to be at somebody's expense.
Society can never think things out.
It has to see them acted out by actors
Devoted actors at a sacrifice—
The ablest actors I can lay my hands on.
Is that your answer?

Whether or not Job would have found such an answer satisfying, Robert Frost makes a point which is not without significance for our own inquiry into the place of the dramatic form in religious presentation.

A more ambitious and for a while remarkably successful play was Archibald Macleish's *J.B.* In a sense it is a play within a play for the two leading characters are broken-down actors, now part of a circus, who decide to play the parts of God and Satan on a side-show stage where others, it seems, have actually been playing the Job-drama. This device enables the playwright to use much of the language of the Book of Job but to give the plot a contemporary reference by presenting a wealthy banker, happy in his marriage and possessing a large family, who by successive strokes of misfortune is reduced to wretchedness, sorrow and penury so that life seems to be utterly unjust and futile. The two actors, wearing the masks of God and Satan, are brought on to the stage at intervals to comment on what is actually happening to the J.B. family. Although they begin in a light-hearted

way, the tension rises as the blows descend until the man behind the Satan mask is screaming abuse against God and
humanity because J.B. is still blessing the God who has
allowed such things to happen – screaming abuse and waiting
for the final collapse when God and man alike will go down in
ruins.

Everything finally hangs on the relationship between J.B. and
Sarah his wife. She stands by him and supports him to the limit –
but at the limit her patience breaks when it seems to her
that J.B. is falling down before a lie, clinging to his slogan
God is just! when in fact there is nothing but injustice, purchas-
ing quiet at the expense of denying the innocence of little
children.

> J.B.: I have no choice but to be guilty.
> SARAH: We have the choice to live or die,
> All of us . . .
> > *curse God and die.*

And she runs soundlessly out of the circle of light. Lower and
lower J.B. sinks, tortured, trampled upon, tempted, crushed.
But he is not extinguished. How then will the end come? For
Macleish the final scene brings Sarah back with a broken twig in
her hand. She fondles the petals of the tree which speaks of
springtime, the forsythia:

> I found it growing in the ashes,
> Gold as though it did not know
> I broke the branch to strip the leaves off—
> Petals again! . . .
> > But they so cling to it.
> J.B.: Curse God and die, you said to me.

SARAH: Yes. You wanted justice, didn't you?
   There isn't any. There's the world . . .
   Cry for justice and the stars
   Will stare until your eyes sting. Weep,
   Enormous winds will thrash the water.
   Cry in sleep for your lost children,
   Snow will fall
        snow will fall.
J.B.: Why did you leave me alone?
SARAH: I loved you
   I couldn't help you any more.
   You wanted justice and there was none —
   Only love.

No summary can give an adequate impression of a play which moves backwards and forwards between the old actors and the J.B. family. On the one side the dialogue between God and Satan is often tense and bitter. On the other side the disasters which can befall a seemingly prosperous family are not exaggerated. The exposure of human suffering is intensely moving, the fortitude of J.B. heroic and convincing. The *dénouement* effected through the return of Sarah may be open to criticism but it is in no way sentimentalised or offered as a cheap resolution. Job's problem — the problem of suffering remains. It cannot be finally resolved in human terms. It is the function of the artist, whether in Palestine or on Broadway, to help us to bear the pain and to see through the darkness of suffering a glimpse of supernatural light.

  Our gaze is submarine, our eyes look upward
  And see the light that fractures through unquiet water.
  We see the light but see not whence it comes.

If the book of Job approximates most closely to the dramatic form, the story of Hosea approaches nearest to dramatic content amongst the writings of the Old Testament. It is akin to the great tragedies of Greece and has been used by Marc Connelly, in the drama to which I have already referred, to bring his play to its climax in the penultimate scene. There Hezdrel, a heroic leader, is encouraging his followers to stand firm against the forces of Herod who is determined to seize the temple, burn its contents and slay its defenders. God comes to him in disguise:

GOD: How is it you is so brave?

HEZDREL: Caize we got faith, dat's why!

GOD: Faith? In who?

HEZDREL: In our dear Lawd God.

GOD: But God say he abandoned ev'one down yere.

HEZDREL: Who say dat? Who dare say dat of de Lawd God of Hosea?

GOD: Who's he?

HEZDREL: De God of mercy.

GOD: How you s'pose Hosea found dat mercy?

HEZDREL: De only way he could find it. De only way I found it. De only way anyone kin find it.

GOD: How's dat?

HEZDREL: Through sufferin'.

And when at the very end of the play God is talking with Gabriel, he returns to this word of Hezdrel.

Did he mean dat even God must suffer?

In the distance a voice cries.

> Oh, look at him! Oh, look, dey goin' to make him
> carry it up dat high hill! Dey goin' to nail him to it!
> Oh, dat's a terrible burden for one man to carry!

[God rises and murmurs 'Yes' as if in recognition. The heavenly beings have been watching him closely, and now, seeing him smile gently, draw back, relieved. All the angels burst into 'Hallelujah, King Jesus'. God continues to smile as the lights fade away. The singing becomes fortissimo.]

Such is the moving re-interpretation of the experience of Hosea through the dramatic adaptation of the meditations of some southern Negro preacher. I would like now to put alongside it the commentary of a brilliant young philosopher of Jewish origin who has translated Yiddish drama into English and has thought deeply about the theme of tragedy and especially about its relation to human suffering. In a key-passage of his book *The Problem of Tragedy* Morris Engel says this:

"Tragedy, to put it briefly, confronts us with the mystery of human suffering and tries to explain it. We respond to the mystery and are elevated by the explanation. The consolation of tragedy is the consolation of attaining some insight into one's grief or distress, and the greater the insight the greater the sense of elation. This is a universal feature of all tragic dramas and lies at the very foundation of the tragic experience.

"Regarded from within, every tragedy consists of two parts: a question and an answer. These two parts cannot always be separated and often neither the question nor the answer is explicitly formulated. But sometimes the question is asked by the tragic hero himself who also supplies the answer. An extreme and early example of this process is the tragedy of Hosea.

"He married, Hosea relates, a woman by the name of Gomer who, he later discovered, had become unfaithful to him. But although her infidelity bore down heavily upon him, he could neither change her ways nor stop loving her. And so he continued to keep her in his house and to care for the children from her licentious unions until, one day, she left him completely for a life of sin and vice which eventually found her the slave concubine of another man. But his love for her – a love which degrades as well as elevates – was so overpowering that he sought her out, redeemed her from slavery and reclaimed her as his lawful wife. Seeking some reason for this madness and passion which filled and tortured his soul and finding none, Hosea turned to see who else in this vast universe loved so deeply and suffered so much, and discovered God. He came to see, he tells us, that his agony was preordained and that his own tragic life was symbolic of the story of the relationship between God and His people Israel. This discovery made his suffering, at last, appear intelligible – even desirable – to him, and was the beginning of his ministry in the service of God. He proclaimed throughout the land that infidelity is the root of all evil and the chief sin of which the people of Israel, the adulterous wife, is guilty against Yahweh, her loving husband, but that in spite of this infidelity, God's infinite love for His people will not allow Him to cast Israel away, just as he, Hosea, could not cast Gomer from his heart. And so from hilltop to hilltop, Hosea, 'the prophet of the sorrowful heart', told the intimate story of his life and pleaded with the people to repent."*

What Hosea experienced inwardly and exteriorised outwardly in this dramatic fashion could be paralleled by appealing to the writings of Jeremiah and Ezekiel. Each of these prophets felt deeply the sorrows and disillusionments of his own people. Each was vividly aware of the iniquities and infidelities which had been rife in the life of the nation. Each employed forms of acted

* *The Problem of Tragedy.* 40 ff.

parables to bring home to the consciences of the exiles the inner truth of their situation. Often this meant an almost intolerable strain. To be identified with them in sympathy and understanding and yet to stand against them in indignation and judgement led to conflicts which almost inevitably worked themselves out in dramatic form. And the supreme expression of this conflict, transcending all others, is that experienced by Jesus Himself and recorded for us in the four Gospels. To the dramatic elements in the witness of the Evangelists I must finally turn.

IV

In the Gospels, it seems to me, we find a double use of the dramatic form. There is first the total drama of Jesus' own earthly career. Secondly there are dramas within the total drama – the dramas which we normally call the parables of Jesus. Some of these are so compressed that their main function is to suggest one vivid point of comparison: the Kingdom of God is like leaven or a mustard seed or a drag-net or a pearl merchant. But a few are extended and take on a definitely dramatic form as they introduce characters related to one another in love or hate, in respect or contempt, in care or unconcern. Let us look at one or two of these.

In an illuminating section of his inaugural lecture as Professor of Drama at Bristol University, Glynne Wickham defined the quintessence of drama as "the mirror of moral values in society – of man's interest in himself, of his regard for his neighbour, and of his respect for his gods". "It is this balance (or lack of balance)," he continued, "in any society which distinguishes one civilisation from another. It is the particular quality and purpose of dramatic art to reflect it." How aptly such a parable as that of the Sheep and the Goats answers to this definition! Or the varying versions of the Faithful and Unfaithful Servants. Or the Parables of the Labourers in the Vineyard and of the Great Feast. Here are dramatic representations of man's inhumanity to man, of man's selfish concern for his own advantage, of man's indifference to the call of the highest. Jesus exposes relentlessly the 'lack of balance' in the society of his own time by holding up a mirror of moral values which may suddenly bring revelation to his hearers if they will only surrender themselves to the dramatic challenge.

Even more powerful are the parables which focus a spotlight on what Kenneth Tynan in a perceptive essay has called *a state of desperation*. "Good drama for me," he writes, "is made up of the thoughts, the words and the gestures that are wrung from human beings on their way to or in or emerging from a state of desperation. A play is an ordered sequence of events that brings one or more of the people in it to a desperate condition which it must always explain and if possible resolve. If the worst that can happen is the hero's being sent down from Oxford, we laugh and the play is a farce; if death is a possibility we are getting close to tragedy. Where there is no desperation, or where the desperation is inadequately motivated, there is no drama."

By this standard what can we say for example of the Parable of the Prodigal Son? In the case of the younger son the steps towards his moment of desperation are vividly portrayed. The break with his father, the journey to a far country, the squandering of his resources, the incidence of the famine, the degradation amongst swine, all lead to a despairing situation in which there must either be the surrender to the darkness of oblivion or the cry for mercy and light. But it is not only the son who is pictured in this state. We are indeed left to imagine the feelings of the father as the son turns his back upon all the influences that have hitherto guided and sustained his life but we see more clearly the state of desperation to which the father approaches when the elder son refuses any kind of recognition to his brother and sulks out his resentment in some isolated corner of his own choosing. If a son reaches the point of begrudging his own brother the chance of starting afresh what more can a father do?

Or there is the Parable of the Good Samaritan. Even more obviously a man is pictured in a state of desperation. In a desolate and remote defile, avoided by potential bearers of succour, stripped of clothing and dangerously wounded, what possible hope is there for such a man? Surely not in the chance approach of a member of an alien race? But it is when all ordinary hopes have been extinguished and death is in sight that the miracle happens. Out of the state of desperation a new hope and together with it a new beauty is born. Or there are the two extremes dramatically represented in the Parable of the Unforgiving Servant. A man is bankrupt, in debt for a sum of staggering dimensions. Every door of escape is closed. And then out of the desperate emergency the man goes forth into freedom and new life. What magnanimity of spirit such an experience will doubtless engender! Will not the forgiven forgive a hundredfold? But by a complete reversal of even human expectancy the second state of desperation is disclosed. The forgiven one is seizing by the throat a man who owes but a trifling sum and demanding immediate payment. What words or gestures are adequate to deal with such a situation? It represents the kind of limiting condition in human affairs with which drama is alone adequate to deal.

I have suggested a few examples of Jesus' use of the dramatic form in his own ministry. But this use was in no way unrelated to the total drama of his earthly career. By means of His dramatic parables, He held up a mirror of moral values to His contemporaries and sought to shock them into a realisation of the desperate situations into which their present policies were leading them. Thoughts and words were wrung from Him as He went forward on His own way to a state of desperation. They symbolised the conflict which was deepening in intensity and was bound to lead ultimately to a crisis of tragic dimensions.

It is remarkable how the opening Act in each Gospel discloses a situation with conflict at its heart and a state of desperation already in view. If we take the section Mark 1. 1–36 we see Jesus wrestling with a violent evil spirit, subduing various diseases, but above all engaged in active and open debate with scribes, Pharisees and Herodians about matters related to their deepest religious convictions. And because Jesus refused to be bound by existing laws and conventions:

"The Pharisees went out and immediately held counsel with the Herodians against Him, how to destroy Him."

Again taking Luke 1. 1–4, 30 we see Jesus when a babe in arms already being designated as the touchstone of an ultimate conflict: at His baptism singled out as one who would winnow humanity and consume the worthless with unquenchable fire: at His temptation struggling on three fronts with the prince of evil: and at Nazareth so violating the exclusive susceptibilities of his fellow countrymen that:

They arose up and put him out of the city and led him to the brow of the hill on which their city was built that they might throw him down headlong.

Here is purpose. Here is conflict. Here is passion – and these are all essential ingredients of the dramatic form. The purpose is expressed through the richly comprehensive term, the Kingdom of God, a term which for Jesus clearly denotes joy and blessedness and reconciliation and fulfilment. Yet in conflict with all that this represents are human narrowness and exclusiveness and conservatism and prejudice. And as Archibald Macleish has penetratingly remarked, "To taste the human tragedy one must taste at the same time the possibility of human happiness, for it is only when the two are known together in a single knowledge that either can be known." Jesus already knew the blessedness of the Kingdom of God and human life through the trustfulness of little children, the processes of growth to perfection in the natural world, the joy of working with those of kindred spirit in a Divine task. But he also knew the frantic clingings to security and struggles for status and yearnings for power that the human scene disclosed. Passionately He longed for the coming of the Kingdom. Passionately He strove to lead men into the Kingdom. So the Hero pursues His way, grasped by the vision of the Kingdom of God, resisted by the engineers of the kingdom of this world – and the drama proceeds to its critical *dénouement*.

In all the Gospels the critical section is that occupied by the Passion Story, beginning with the events of the first Palm Sunday and continuing through to the first Easter Day. But in the Gospel of Mark the tension is already heightening by the time the eighth chapter is reached. After the first Act, to which I have already referred, comes a second dealing mainly with Jesus' teaching and works of healing. Then at 8. 31 the atmosphere suddenly changes. "He began to teach them that the Son of man must suffer many things." And the third Act is interspersed with references to taking up the cross, being delivered into the hands of men, leaving all, being persecuted, drinking a cup, giving up one's life, rising from the dead. We are made aware of a dread possibility lying ahead and then with the entry into Jerusalem the days of crisis begin. There are tense debates. There is the clash in the temple courts. There is the searing parable about the husbandmen who rejected the owner's messengers and finally murdered his son. There is an apocalypse telling of impending doom.

Then at last in Chapter 14 we reach the eve of the final conflict. Successive scenes are presented with economy, with restraint and yet with almost unendurable poignancy. The anointing of the body, the preparations for the Passover Meal, the Supper itself, the intense drama of Gethsemane, the trial, the journey to Calvary, the darkness and dereliction of Golgotha – the sequence is so truly dramatic that later writers have needed to make little or no adaptation as they have sought to create passion-plays or passion-music for their own times. It is true that there are certain marked characteristics which distinguish the Matthean and Lukan presentations from that of Mark. An almost royal dignity shines through the Matthean narrative; a noble compassion for other sufferers through the Lukan. The main sequence of the forward march of events remains unaltered but we do not feel the clash of external forces and the intensity of the internal struggle in quite the same way as we do in the Markan account. For each, the passion and death of Jesus are utterly central. Yet each by setting these events within his own particular cultural setting helps to build up the total picture of that which is the crisis of all the ages, the universal criterion of judgement of all peoples.

The plan of the Fourth Gospel is different from that of the Synoptics though the section of the Passion narrative which stretches from the arrest in the garden to the death on the cross follows the same general pattern. What seems to me most distinctive about this Gospel as a whole is the extraordinary way in which the evangelist, as in Greek tragedy, succeeds in giving his readers (originally, of course, the *hearers* of the narrative) the sense of an overwhelmingly mysterious and purposeful Divine

Producer who is directing events forward to their final *dénouement*. On the stage immediately before us the hero plays his characteristic part at Jordan, in Nazareth, in Samaria, in Jerusalem. The scenes have a complete naturalness and spontaneity and fascination of their own. But behind all a majestic plan is in the course of being fulfilled. It is a design which in many ways runs counter to Jesus' own human feelings and instinctive desires. Certainly it cuts clean across the outlook and ambitions of the society to which He belongs. So the struggle grows in intensity:

Now is my soul troubled. And what shall I say?
Father save me from this hour?
No for this purpose I have come to this hour.
Father glorify thy name!

Now is the crisis of this world, now shall the ruler of this world be cast out; and I when I am lifted up from the earth will draw all men to myself.

Only through the appearance on the stage of history of one in whom the Divine judgement on the sin of the world could work itself out to the very limit, only through the action of one who was ready to take the pain and suffering which sin involves upon himself and in so doing to absorb it, only, that is to say, through a death accepted in the face of its horror and seeming finality, only thus could the grim entail of the world's evil be broken and men be redeemed from their alienation from the life of God.

So the drama of the ages is played out on the stage of a small province of the Roman Empire in the first century of our era. We see the clash of forces, we hear the battle of words. The ultimate result on the human plane is never really in doubt. Yet the central figure goes forward with steadfast determination though not without apprehension, upheld by the assurance that He is fulfilling a Divine purpose however mysterious it may seem to mortal eyes. The cry from the cross recorded only by the fourth evangelist sums up the tragedy and leaves us, the spectators, still free to make our ultimate response. "It is finished" – to some this must stand as the final verdict on the meaningless suffering of an innocent man. "It is finished" – to others this stands as the final vindication of the ways of God who through taking suffering into His own being bears away the sin of the world.

By a wonderful providence four examples of early Passion drama have been preserved for later ages and constitute one of our most precious cultural possessions. But in the time of their provenance they were not intended for private reading and meditation. Rather, it seems, their main use was to be for reciting at the times when the Christian fellowship assembled for the breaking of the bread. On these occasions the traditional actions associated with the bread and the cup were set within the wider context of the temple-ministry, the arrest and trial and the actual crucifixion of the Lord. They remembered the deliverance which He wrought on their behalf, the new covenant inaugurated through the shedding of His own life blood. And they offered their sacrifice of thanksgiving in dramatic form by repeating His actions with bread and cup and by sharing with one another the tokens of His passion. The dramatic action retained its character of objectivity in that it celebrated what Christ Himself had done on man's behalf. At the same time it brought men into an experience of subjective identification with Him as they together ate the bread and drank the cup which He had provided for them. So the drama of salvation was constantly re-enacted. Not only were the participants' motives and feelings cleansed: their whole being was sanctified and renewed by sharing in the dramatic experience. As often as they ate the bread and drank the cup they recited the dramatic story of the Lord's Passion as the verbal accompaniment to their actions. And by the very performance of the total drama they 'showed forth', proclaimed the Lord's death, 'till He comes'.

V

As I draw to the end of this brief excursion into the realm of Biblical drama I find myself returning in mind to the magisterial opening words of the Epistle to the Hebrews:

God, who at sundry times and in divers manners spake in time past to the fathers by the prophets, hath in these last days spoken to us by a Son, whom he appointed heir of all things, by whom also he made the worlds. When He who is the effulgence of God's splendour and the stamp of God's very being, had made purification for our sins He sat down at the right hand of the majesty on high.

Here in summary form is the essential drama of salvation. 'Spake', 'spoken', need not be restricted to purely verbal formulations. They surely include such dramas as we have considered. in this book, the complex of setting, words and actions presented through the stories of Abraham, Moses, Hosea and many another. Each of these dramas is an integral part of the total drama which reaches its climax of revelation and action in the story of the Passion of Him who is confessed to be the Son of God. Taking our analogy from common human experience we can imagine God as author of the play, as producer of the scenes played out by human actors, as himself assuming the central role in the climactic act which integrates and gives meaning to the whole. Further we can imagine the drama continuing to be re-enacted in the moral and aesthetic experience of the Christian fellowship, with outstanding occasions when the drama is played out with singular intensity and impelling conviction. Through artistic re-presentation and through ethical re-interpretation the drama makes its impression upon successive generations. And still at sundry times and in divers places men and women renounce the role of mere spectator and joyfully yield themselves up to participation in the ongoing dramatic action.

No analogy is perfect but I can at least suggest one example of what I have in mind. One of the most beautiful and moving books that I have encountered in recent years is entitled *The Passion in Africa*. It is the record through words and photographs of an experiment initiated by Canon John V. Taylor when he was living and working as a missionary in Uganda. In an African setting, using Negro spirituals as choral accompaniments, members of an African Christian community re-enacted the drama of the Passion of our Lord. The photographs themselves bear witness to the devotion of those who participated in the play and to the care with which each performed his part. And the author in his introduction tells us how, through their very involvement in the dramatic experience, one and another gained a deeper apprehension of and a deeper commitment to that which had already become in a measure familiar through spoken and written words.

Seeking to draw out the theological implications of the total experiment and experience Dr. Taylor says this:

"Without a regular, corporate experience of the drama of the Christian story it is doubtful whether Christianity can ever lay firm hold upon any community. If the Faith is to become really established in African soil it must push its roots below the strata of institutional acceptance and intellectual understanding, down into the deeper levels of imagination and symbolism and the unconscious rhythm of life.

"For the Christian Faith is a drama. Indeed, for those who are its captives, it is seen to be *the* drama which embraces and fulfils all man's profoundest insights, and of which all the great dramatic myths are an echo. Here is the tragedy of Man, the archetype from which all the great tragedies of the playwrights derive their universal truth. Here is the supreme human suspense, the promise of deliverance, the slow centuries of expectancy, the cry, O Lord, how long?, and then the staggering surprise and perfection of the fulfilment at Bethlehem. Here, above all, is the drama of God: the purpose gradually unfolded, act after act, progressing always out of frustration, every broken thread woven into the pattern, every ruin built patiently into the rising structure, until the final defeat, the rejection and murder of the incarnate God, lets loose in the world the irresistible power of a Redeemer-Creator whose love must make all things new."

No words of my own could more adequately summarise the theme which I have tried to present in this book by looking again at dramas, Biblical and modern, which seem to me to be integral parts of the one great drama of Salvation.